Questions Children Ask

& How to Answer Them

DR. MIRIAM STOPPARD

Questions Children Ask

& How to Answer Them

DK PUBLISHING, INC.

For Ol, Barney, Will, Ed, Oona,
Slater and Tiberio

A DK PUBLISHING BOOK

ILLUSTRATED BY
CAROLINE EWEN

Managing Editor
Jemima Dunne

Managing Art Editor
Phil Gilderdale

Project Editor
Nicky Adamson

Senior Art Editor
Karen Ward

Designers
Luke Herriott
Maria Wheatley

Production
Antony Heller

Photography
Steve Gorton

First American Edition, 1997
2 4 6 8 10 9 7 5 3 1

Published in the United States by
DK Publishing, Inc., 95 Madison Avenue
New York, New York 10016

Visit us on the World Wide Web at http://www.dk.com

Library of Congress Cataloging-in-Publication Data
Stoppard, Miriam.
Questions children ask / by Miriam Stoppard. -- 1st Amer. ed.
p. cm.
Includes index.
ISBN 0-7894-1471-6
1. Children's questions and answers. 2. Child psychology.
3. Child rearing. I. Title
HQ784.Q4S76 1996
649'.1--dc20 96–33599 CIP

Reproduced in Hong Kong by Bright Arts
Printed and bound in Italy by Interlitho, Milan

CONTENTS

"How does the baby get out?"

"What happens when you die?"

"Do I have to call him daddy?"

"Why isn't my skin brown?"

"What does violence mean?"

INTRODUCTION

Writing this book has been prompted by many things, the first being my belief that children must be told the truth. This is the parents' dilemma: when facing a sensitive question, you may wish to give a truthful response but feel that your children aren't ready for the details. You'd be right on both counts, but instead of copping out, or giving a sanitized version, you can opt to provide the amount of truth your child can deal with. Children are naturally curious. From the moment they can formulate questions – at about two years of age – they will continue to bombard their parents with "Why?" "What?" "Where?" and "How?" But it is one thing to find an answer to "How do cars work?" It is quite another if the question is, "Where did I come from?" Telling the truth doesn't mean telling all, it means starting with simple facts, and adding in more knowledge as your child grows up and can handle more complex information. For instance, few children can cope with the mechanics of sex before the age of eight. Some will be much older. It's useless to burden your child with sophisticated explanations when simpler ones would have been satisfactory. When a child is mentally and emotionally ready for information, it's never embarrassing to give it. Your child is eager for clarifications of matters that are mysterious and confusing. To respond to a child so focused should dispel most parents' diffidence, so timing is crucial.

DEVELOPING MUTUAL TRUST

Many parents believe that in tackling the facts of life, the genders must be segregated, so Dad handles the boys and Mom the girls. This seems the natural order of things, but it carries little conviction if one parent is easygoing and the other is uptight. If you put yourself in your child's position, it's clearly best that the parent who is more comfortable answering children's questions should shoulder the responsibility regardless of gender. To me, keeping the channels of communication open throughout childhood

and into adolescence is one of the most important roles of parents, and it is parents who must make the effort, not children. Who else would you want your children to turn to when they need information, help, advice, and counsel? Yet parents continue to be flabbergasted when, as teenagers, their children become introspective and uncommunicative. While adolescent mood changes are inevitable, children whose early questions have been ignored or deflected are more likely to cut themselves off when really difficult questions arise.

ENCOURAGING A HEALTHY DIALOGUE

Parents whose responses are dismissive or furtive to controversial questions not only make it difficult to raise subjects like race, sex, religion, or drugs within the family – they encourage their children to be furtive themselves. Parents who are open, responsive, and frank encourage self-esteem, balance, and fairness in their children and give them the space to think, weigh options, and decide and act responsibly. This healthy dialogue between parents and children has to begin early – from the very first question – and should continue throughout the entire time they are at home. That is why the answers I suggest start at the earliest age a child may begin asking questions. You are your children's first educators, and all their learning – including sex education – starts at home. Parents find themselves wondering if information, especially about sex or drugs, can harm their children, and they may hold back for fear that giving facts could encourage them to experiment. Nothing could be further from the truth. It's children who don't have information who explore and experiment dangerously. Contrary to what many people fear, children who have been given information about sex are not prurient, don't focus on sex or embark on early experimentation, but keep it in perspective as a normal part of life. There is plenty of research to show that good sex education does not encourage irresponsible behavior; in fact, the exact opposite is true. Parents make it impossible for a child to act responsibly if they withhold information; this applies equally to other subjects generally seen as controversial, such as drugs, alcohol, and smoking, or issues of potential prejudice, such as racial or religious differences.

THE RIGHT ANSWER FOR YOUR CHILD'S AGE

No one, however, can say that being frank and honest is always easy. There are undoubtedly going to be difficult moments when words are hard to find and explanations are elusive. That is why I felt it would be helpful to write this book: I aimed not to supply advice by rote but to give a framework on which you can build your own answers as your child's understanding expands. I have given answers that are suitable for four age groups – ages 2–4, 4–6, 6–8, and 8–11. But none of these age bands is definitive. Children advance and learn at different rates, so look on the bands as a guide – depending on the subject, a very bright child of 3½ might understand the answers given for ages 4–6, while a socially immature boy of nine might be better served by the answers in the band for 6–8-year-olds. I've also written my answers so that they are suitable for both boys and girls, and to emphasize this I have alternated the sex of the child being referred to in my background information question by question, except where for obvious reasons the topics are specifically aimed at girls or boys.

As you read the answers to big questions like, "Where did I come from?" (see page 12), you'll see that the answers for successive age bands become more detailed and complex. If an older child asks a question for the first time, or an alternative version of it, you can give all the preceding information, as well as what's in the answer for your child's own age band. The idea is to choose what you need to help you provide honest, clear answers within what you judge to be the scope of your child's understanding, depending on age and maturity.

PREPARING YOUR ANSWERS

It would be wise, I think, for all but the most self-possessed parent to read over all the background information presented on the topic, including the cross-references. Not that you need to give it all, of course, but it may enable you to answer more confidently if you understand the possible motivation behind your child's line of questioning. This is particularly important for issues of child protection, where you may need to recognize the danger signals behind your child's inquiries. Equally, it could help you to defuse challenging questions from children who may have picked up half-truths. It may even help you to be clearer in your own mind on some subjects if you read the text before formulating an answer for your child. This book is also designed for sharing with your child. It is illustrated with cartoons, diagrams, and pictures that you can look at together, in very much the same close way you might flip through a bedtime story or schoolbook. So the book is at one and the same time designed for parents to read alone and for children and parents to read together, making it easier, I hope, for you and your family to navigate a comfortable route together through even the trickiest questions. To no child is my whole answer necessary. Pick and choose; discard and invent; reject and create. Use examples that are well known to your family in constructing answers; for instance, when describing a certain length of time to a young child, talk about a similar time span between important family events. Explain your own feelings; this is something that your children will value most. Leaven your answers with what you felt and did when you were a child, and you will become more approachable, understanding, and sympathetic in their eyes.

A FOUNDATION FOR THE FUTURE

Look at answering each of your child's questions as an opportunity to teach – not in any formal way, but the kind of teaching that every parent can pass on to children, long before they go to school; the lessons of kindness, tolerance, justice, and generosity. We can socialize our children when they're very young, instilling in them everything from table manners to sexual awareness and moral values. Children have in place a clear understanding of these values (or their opposites) long before they reach the age of five, which means that you as parents are your child's most important teacher and friend – and always will be if you start off right. These are roles and responsibilities you can't refuse. And of course all the effort is worth it, because what comes back is trust, respect and love. I know of few other ways of earning these precious gifts from our children. Every time you look your children straight in the eye, speak with sincerity, and give an honest answer, you bond with them. And those bonds will last throughout life.

Miriam Stoppard

QUESTIONS ABOUT

What's puberty?

Can men have babies?

How does the baby get in there?

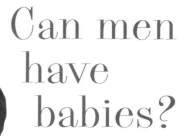

Why have I got a penis?

What is a period?

How are babies made?

How can you tell if someone is gay?

CONCEPTION ● PREGNANCY ● BIRTH ● SEXUAL DEVELOPMENT ●

SEX & BIRTH

All children are curious about themselves and where they came from. As they become aware of their own bodies, they soon register the difference between the sexes. As they grow older, it becomes increasingly difficult to shield them from sexual ideas in the media, and the result of all this is that they will inevitably ask questions about sex. Like

What's a womb?

many parents, you may dread these questions, but try not to duck the issue because you are embarrassed. Sex may have been a taboo in your family, but your young children haven't been programmed as you were. Their interest comes from their natural curiosity and desire to learn, so answering their questions honestly and sympathetically is a way of loving and respecting them. Use the answers here to help you respond truthfully to questions about sex, in a way that is appropriate to your child's age and maturity. Remember that few children below the age of eight can understand the mechanics of sex. Always try to include love, emotions, feelings, and values in any discussion involving sex. If you combine these with honesty and openness, you will help your children develop self-control and judgment about sexual behavior in the future.

Why was I born?

Q Where did I come from?

- *How are babies made?* ● *Why was I born?*

- *Did a stork bring me/Was I found in a cabbage patch?*

- *What is "pregnant"?* ● *How does the baby get in there?*

This is frequently the first question a small child ever asks about the facts of life. In an older child, it's a sign that he's beginning to have some understanding of his uniqueness as a person, but after the age of six the question may rapidly be superseded by the more knowing, "What is sex?"

WHAT'S BEHIND THIS QUESTION

The world of a young child is very self-centered and a simple answer will satisfy his curiosity. Questions often arise when you tell your child that you are expecting another baby, and this is a crucial time to be ready to answer questions about sex, reproduction, and the development of a pregnancy.

If you aren't pregnant, but an older child begins to ask questions like these, it may be because he has seen something about babies at school, on TV, or in a magazine or newspaper. Children over six are genuinely interested in these quite profound questions.

GUIDELINES FOR YOUR ANSWERS

- Don't shrink from the truth. You owe your child an honest and open answer without showing any fear or embarrassment.
- Don't feel you have give every single detail to a young child: It's not necessary, and it's not good for your child, who may be frightened by what he can't grasp. After about the age of eight, most children are capable of understanding the mechanics of sex.

- To be sure you are answering your child's question, paraphrase it: "Do you want to know how you were made when you were a baby?"
- Don't over-complicate: Your six-year-old may pose the question and you find yourself embarking on a long, detailed answer, after which your child says, "No. John said he was from New Jersey; where am I from?"

WHAT ELSE TO KNOW

- With increasing age your child needs answers of increasing complexity, but without extraneous detail. Try to use words your child already understands so no further explanation is necessary.
- Remember that children are very literal. If you talk about planting a seed, they may ask how you water it and what color the flower will be!
- Although very young children usually accept simple explanations at face value, children over five or six often react with a "Yuck!" on first hearing about anything sexual. This is a clear sign that are not ready to learn about sex in any more detail. In fact, it is very healthy. Change the subject and try another time.

Other things you may be asked

- *Are all babies made like that?*
- *What's Mommy's egg/Daddy's seed?*
- *Do Daddies make boys and Mommies make girls?*
- *Can men have babies?*

See also *What is sex? p. 18* ● *What's a vagina? p. 20* ● *What's a penis? p. 22*

A You were made in your Mommy's tummy and you grew in there safely until it was time for you to be born.

A You were made from a seed from Daddy and an egg from Mommy. Daddy's seed and Mommy's egg joined together in Mommy's tummy to make you, so you're half made up of Daddy and half made up of Mommy. You're a very special person and a wonderful mixture of Mommy and Daddy.

A Daddy's seeds, which are called sperm, are made in his testes, which are inside the special pounch of skin, called a scrotum, hanging behind his penis. Millions of tiny sperm are being made there all the time, and they are mixed with a white liquid called semen.

Mommy's eggs grow inside her body in two egg-makers called ovaries. Every month Mommy's ovaries make an egg. When Mommy and Daddy made you, semen from Daddy's penis carried the sperm into Mommy's womb. Just one of the millions of sperm joined up with Mummy's egg to start a new baby – you!

A You are here because Mom and Dad love each other and wanted to have a baby. To make a baby, Dad put his penis into Mom's vagina during sexual intercourse, and semen containing millions and millions of tiny sperm – about 100 million sperm in one teaspoon of semen – traveled up the vagina and through the womb, in the lower part of Mom's tummy, to join her egg. The scientific names for the egg and womb are "ovum" and "uterus." The sperm swam very fast by lashing their long tails. To make sure you would be strong and healthy, the fastest sperm joined up with the ovum to create the beginning of a new baby. While a baby is growing in the uterus, a woman is said to be pregnant. It takes about nine months (40 weeks), for a baby to grow big enough to be born. Men can't have babies, because they don't have wombs. Whether a baby is a boy or a girl depends on which sperm joins the egg, because some sperm make boys and others make girls. Usually, no one knows which kind of sperm has won the race until the baby is born. That's why it is so exciting when the baby comes out and we can find out if it is a boy or a girl!

Q Does the baby grow inside you?

- *How does the baby live in your tummy?*
- *Why doesn't it fall out?* • *What does the baby do in your tummy?*
- *How does it breathe in your tummy?* • *What does it eat?*

Children are intrigued by the way a fetus develops in the womb – once they know it's there, they are just as fascinated by its progress as adults are. If you are expecting a new baby, you can help your older children share the experience as soon as the questions arise. Give them as much information as possible at every stage of the pregnancy, at the right level for their age and understanding.

WHAT'S BEHIND THIS QUESTION

A small child is simply trying to get a fix on a baby who's apparently locked away inside someone's body. It may be an addition to your family, or that of a friend – or your child may just have noticed a heavily pregnant woman in the supermarket, say, or at the doctor's.

These questions often go hand in hand with those on the previous pages, particularly "How does the baby get in there?" Young children are usually quite satisfied with a simple answer. An older child will be curious about the things that particularly interest him – like what the baby eats or drinks, and whether it can breathe, see, or hear. Children over six may have begun to learn about these things at school in science and will be eager to apply their own knowledge to this unseen person.

GUIDELINES FOR YOUR ANSWERS

- This is an opportunity for a simple anatomy lesson. Use the illustrations here to help you explain how a baby grows and develops in the uterus.
- It's best to begin with broad strokes with a child under eight. You can gradually introduce more complex explanations with your eight- to ten-year-old.

- It's reassuring to use a wall chart or pregnancy book with month-by-month illustrations to show your child how a fetus develops as the weeks go by. Position the chart on the wall at your child's eye level so that it can be used as a reference at any time. An eight- or ten-year-old could be shown in more detail in a book.
- Whatever the age of your child, stress the fact that the unborn baby is happy, warm, content, well fed, and can move around within a few weeks of implantation in the uterus. If the baby is a new sibling-to-be, the goal is to help your child develop a relationship with the unborn baby so that he or she will be loved and welcomed when born. This way you can help the older child not to feel replaced or jealous.
- Encourage a small child to rest his head near your tummy. Say things like, "I'm cuddling both my children now." This will help your child get used to the idea of another person in the family well before the time of the birth, and it will encourage him to accept the new baby more readily after he or she is born.

WHAT ELSE TO KNOW

- Talk to children about a forthcoming new baby all the time as "your baby," so that they can feel that the new baby belongs just as much to them as to you, the parents. This will encourage a feeling of protection and ownership before the baby is born.
- Choose a name together, as a family.
- Let your child feel the baby kick, and take him with you to prenatal checkups so that he can hear the heartbeat or even see the ultrasound (sonogram) as well.

Other things you may be asked...

- *Is it dark in your tummy?*
- *Does the baby move around?*
- *Can the baby see/hear anything in there?*
- *How big is the baby in your tummy?*

See also *Where did I come from? p. 12* • *How does the baby get out? p. 16*

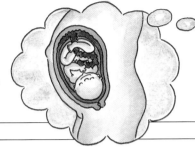

A Your baby has its own special nest in Mommy's tummy. It is very warm and cozy, and the baby is safe and happy.

A Your baby grows in a special bag, called a womb, which is inside Mommy's tummy. It starts very small, but bit by bit, it grows arms and legs, eyes, nose, and mouth, just like you. Your baby is so happy it kicks, sucks its thumb, opens and closes its eyes, or listens to the gurgles in Mommy's tummy. And sometimes it just rests, too.

A When the baby in the womb is a month old, it is the size of your thumbnail. Its heart is beating by the time it is six weeks old! Its brain is forming, too. The baby's arms and legs start from little buds, and by 12 weeks it will have fingers and toes and it looks like a tiny human – but it's only about the length of my index finger. It takes a long time – nine whole months – for a baby to grow big enough to be born. It doesn't need to eat, drink, or breathe because food and oxygen come to it through a special cord attached to its tummy, and connected to its mother, in the womb.

A When a father's sperm joins a mother's ovum the fertilized egg is the size of a pinhead, but it only takes about three months in the uterus for it to begin to look like a real baby. During these early weeks the fetus goes through stages where it seems to have gills like a fish and a little tail like a monkey. These are thought to be signs that humans evolved from sea creatures and then from apes. The baby's food and drink come from the mother's blood and it reaches the baby through the umbilical cord. Your belly button shows where your cord was when you were a baby inside Mom. The cord leads to a part of the uterus called the placenta that allows the baby's and mother's blood to mix, so the baby gets food and oxygen and can get rid of carbon dioxide – the part of the air we breathe that we don't need.

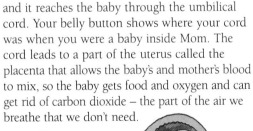
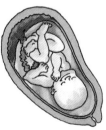
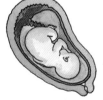

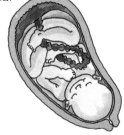

The fetus at 4 weeks – ⅙ in (4 mm)

At about 12 weeks – 3½ in (9 cm)

At about 20 weeks – 7⅙ in (18.5 cm)

At about 32 weeks – 12 in (32 cm)

At about 40 weeks and ready to be born – 19-21 in (52-56 cm)

How does the baby get out?

- *How does the baby know when to be born?*
- *Does a doctor get the baby out?* • *Where does the baby come out?*
- *What happens when the baby is born?*

Children are as fascinated by the process of birth as adults, but they'll have little or no idea of how it all works. The younger they are, the more likely that they will accept simple explanations, but if you are going to a hospital to give birth and your child will not be with you, you should be very clear about when you and the new baby will be returning home.

WHAT'S BEHIND THIS QUESTION

All children try to guess how the baby will come out – small children think that perhaps a mother will "unzip!" Older children are interested in the mechanics of birth – they may ask to see the hole where the baby comes out. Some children could well have seen animals such as puppies or kittens being born either at your home or a friend's, or on television, and may want to know if it is the same for people. Older children who have some knowledge of human biology may also want to know whether it hurts the mother and how it affects the baby.

GUIDELINES FOR YOUR ANSWERS

Try to be as accurate as possible, particularly if you are the parents-to-be. If you've decided to have your baby in the hospital, entailing an enforced absence from your older child or children, it is important to let them know that you are not going to disappear forever, and that the time before they can see you again will be short. That's why it's worth explaining the stages of labor with your child so she has an idea of what will be happening when, and will understand that it could take a little while. Whether the questions arise because you or someone close to your child is pregnant, or whether the subject comes up simply from curiosity, use the illustrations here or in a pregnancy manual to help explain what happens. Try not to alarm your child with talk of pain and long labors.

If you know of a pet cat or dog about to give birth, try to take your child to see it either at, or immediately after, the birth of the kittens or puppies. Then make it clear that your child is welcome to come and see you and her new baby in the hospital as soon as possible after the birth, if she wants to.

WHAT ELSE TO KNOW

- If possible, take your child to the hospital before the birth and show her the rooms for patients and the nursery so that she has a picture of where you will be.
- Let your child join in your preparation exercises. It makes it more fun for everyone and you can use them to help her understand what's happening.
- If your child wants to see where the baby will come out, explain that the hole is too small. Show your child a picture instead.
- If you choose to have your baby at home, make sure that you involve older children in the preparations. Don't exclude them from the birth if you all feel happy about it and there is no emergency. Discuss this in advance with your doctor or midwife.

Other things you may be asked...

- *Does it hurt to have a baby?*
- *How long does it take to be born?*
- *Will you still love me when the baby is born?*
- *Will the baby have hair and teeth?*
- *Why do you have to go to the hospital?*

See also *Where did I come from? p. 12* • *Does the baby grow inside you? p. 14*

FOR AGES 2–4

A After a while, the baby is too big for Mommy's tummy, so it has to be born. I'll love you both then.

FOR AGES 4–6

A Your baby is ready to be born when it needs more food than it can get from Mommy and it's too big to fit inside Mommy anymore. Daddy's taking me to the hospital so the baby is born safely. Grandma will look after you, and Daddy will bring you to see me tomorrow. We'll all be at home in a couple of days with your new baby. I'll always love you.

FOR AGES 6–8

A The womb is normally closed to keep the baby safe, but when the baby is ready to be born the bottom of the womb – called the cervix – slowly stretches open, like elastic, and the strong womb muscles push the baby down the vagina and out from between Mommy's legs. This takes a few hours to happen. Nearly all human babies are born this way, and quite a few other baby animals, too. When the baby is born, he or she will probably cry a little and will look around for the first time. Some babies have lots of hair, some only a little, and most babies don't grow teeth until they're about six months old.

FOR AGES 8–11

A The baby knows when it is time to be born when it grows too big for the amount of food coming from its mother. And the mother's body knows, too, because the baby is getting too big to fit inside. The way out of the uterus is at its bottom, through the cervix, which is shut tight during pregnancy. When the baby is ready to be born, the muscles of the uterus stretch the cervix open and push the baby down through the vagina – known as the birth canal. Because the muscles are so strong, it can be painful for the mother. The time when a baby is being pushed out is called "labor," which means work, because having a baby is hard work for the mother. Labor can last as much as 18 hours or longer, because the birth canal stretches very slowly so that it isn't damaged. Women having babies are cared for by doctors, nurses, or midwives. After the birth the pains stop, and the vagina and womb shrink back to their normal size.

Q What is sex?

- *What is sexual intercourse?* • *What is making love?*
- *Do you (Mommy and Daddy) have sex?*
- *Why do people have sex?* • *Will I ever have sex?*

This is the one question that will inevitably be asked and which you should be ready to answer truthfully, whatever the age of your child. Being ready to answer your child's questions about sexual intercourse will help foster a responsible and healthy attitude toward sex when your child is old enough to be sexually active.

WHAT'S BEHIND THIS QUESTION

Few very young children ask this question unless they witness something overt, perhaps by wandering into the bedroom while you are making love – and then the question would simply be "What are you doing?" If a very young child does ask some of the questions above, it may be a danger sign of possible abuse (see p. 78), or it may simply mean that he has been listening to older children. An older child asks these questions for three probable reasons:

- He may have heard or read the words "sex," "sexual intercourse," "making love," or similar, and is naturally curious. Your child wants a definition.
- Your child may have seen some aspect of sexual behavior in a newspaper or magazine photograph, on TV or in a movie or video. Again, your child may simply be curious, or possibly slightly alarmed, depending on the context of what he or she has seen, so find out the background circumstances.
- Your child may have picked up the idea that sex is a difficult or embarrassing subject for adults and that they don't want to talk to children about it. Then the questions are challenging; stay cool.

Whether challenging or fact-finding, don't shy away from this question; instead, try to anticipate your child's concerns. Demystifying sex is the best way to avoid its becoming the object of furtive or "dirty" talk.

GUIDELINES FOR YOUR ANSWERS

- This question should always be looked at along with the next two (*What's a vagina?* p. 20, and *What's a penis?* p. 22), since they are all very closely related. Choose your answers according to your child's needs.
- Answering questions such as these provides an opportunity to emphasize to children that sex should come from love and with love comes responsibility: the responsibility to put the other person before themselves, never to coerce, pressure, or force, and to have respect for others and for themselves.
- Preschool children need only the simplest explanations about sex. While you may be trembling in anticipation of the next question, they will just change the subject or say "Thanks," and run off to play.

WHAT ELSE TO KNOW

- Think of each question your child asks as an opportunity to convey your standards and values and to help your child feel loved and well informed.
- There's rarely a need for detailed information about the mechanics of sex for a child under eight.
- Try to anticipate your child's concerns. Remember that sex is also about self-control and abstinence, and you should school your child in these qualities.

Other things you may be asked

- *Why would anybody want to have sex?*
- *Do you make a baby every time you have sex?*
- *Do you only have sex in bed?*
- *Why do people kiss and cuddle?*
- *Do you stop having sex when you're old?*

See also *Where did I come from? p. 12* • *What's a vagina? p. 20* • *What's a penis? p. 22* • *What's a contraceptive? p. 30*

Sex is a sort of cuddling that Mommies and Daddies do to show how much they love each other.

Sex is one way that two grown-ups who love each other, like Mommy and Daddy, can be as close as possible to cuddle and kiss in a special way, usually in bed. Sometimes a man and woman can start a baby when they have sex.

Sex is one of the ways in which two grown-up people can show that they love each other very much. Sex is the time when they can make each other feel happy and wonderful. When we talk about sex in this way it is short for "sexual intercourse." During sexual intercourse, a man's penis gets stiff and he puts it inside a woman's vagina, which feels good. Having sex can start a baby if the man and the woman want it to, but it usually doesn't because grown-ups generally have sex as a way of showing how much they love each other – even when they are quite old.

Your sex can mean whether you are a girl or a boy – your "gender." But sex is also short for "sexual intercourse," which is how grown-ups like Mom and Dad can make someone they love feel very happy and good about themselves – that's why we call it making love. During sexual intercourse, a man puts his penis inside a woman's vagina, and they feel good. The feeling becomes more and more exciting until it reaches a climax, when the man's sperm spurts – or ejaculates – into the woman's vagina. You don't have to take your clothes off, but most people like to because it helps to get really close, so sex happens most often in bed when two people don't wear clothes. There are lots of different ways that two people can have sex, as long as it is comfortable for both of them. Although having sexual intercourse can make a baby, many people have sex simply because they love each other and it feels good, so they use contraceptives that prevent a baby from starting. People usually wait until they are grown up before they begin having sexual relationships, but no one should have sex with anyone else until they feel they are ready for it.

Q What's a vagina?

- *What's a vagina for?* ● *Why haven't I got a penis?*
- *What's a penis for?* ● *Why don't boys have a vagina?*
- *When will I be able to have a baby?* ● *What are breasts for?*

All children want to identify with other children of the same gender. They are concerned not to be taken for the opposite gender, so they want to know about all similarities and all differences. Girls want to know about the things that are special to them. But boys also need to know, so if you can, discuss the answers here and those for "What's a penis?" (p. 22) with both sons and daughters together, so that each gender knows about the other.

WHAT'S BEHIND THIS QUESTION

Girls start to identify with other girl children from an early age, and will look for signs of similarity between girls and features that distinguish them from boys. However, very few girls under the age of four will be interested enough to ask questions, mainly because they think everybody else is made the way they are. From school age on, girls begin to look for differences between children and between grown men and women.

The presence of a penis is such an obvious yardstick that children use it naturally as a way of distinguishing between the sexes: "Is this doll a girl or a boy? Where's the penis?" There's no harm in a mother showing her daughter that she doesn't have a penis; it is the best kind of reassurance and will make your daughter feel confident about herself – she is the same as Mommy! Equally, a daughter will often compare herself with her father, note the differences, and want to know why.

GUIDELINES FOR YOUR ANSWERS

● Don't ever scold your child for being sexually curious about the opposite sex; satisfy that curiosity by answering questions frankly and honestly.

● Much was once made of the Freudian theory that girls suffer from "penis envy" – that they are innately jealous that they do not have a penis. This may not be literally true, but girls do have to wait a long time before developing visible signs of their own sexuality – their breasts. But they have two – a source of pride.

● If you have sons as well as daughters, include them in your conversation. Boys need to know about girls because knowledge and understanding will help instill in them a sense of responsibility and understanding of girls' and women's needs from an early age.

WHAT ELSE TO KNOW

● Any girl will explore herself during her first and second years. This is part of normal childhood development. Be tolerant and never ask your baby to refrain from touching herself – accept that it is normal and pleasurable. It isn't "dirty."

● Your daughter may start asking specifically about sex from the age of six; she may play "Mommies and Daddies" when she imitates you, and may want to explore boys' bodies. Relax; this is normal, but keep an eye on it to make sure it is safe.

● Your nine- to ten-year-old daughter could become shy about asking questions, so encourage her to speak frankly: mothers particularly should try to be open with their growing daughters. Tell her what developing as a woman was like for you.

Other things you may be asked...

- ■ *Do boys have breasts?*
- ■ *Does urine come out of the vagina?*
- ■ *What's a clitoris?*
- ■ *When did you/Mom get your/her breasts?*
- ■ *What are ovaries?*
- ■ *What's a womb?*

See also *Where did I come from? p. 12* ● *What is sex? p. 18* ● *What's a penis? p. 22* ● *What does puberty mean? p. 26*

FOR AGES 2-4

Few children under the age of four will ask this question because they take their anatomy for granted. But if your child does begin to notice and ask about gender differences, base your answers on those given for the 4–6 age group below.

FOR AGES 4-6

A The vagina is a tube that goes up into your body from the opening between your legs. Boys and men don't have vaginas; they have penises. When a girl grows up, the vagina is the tube that male seeds travel along to make a baby. The vagina stretches so the baby can come out when it is born. Breasts are for making milk to feed a newborn baby. You'll start getting breasts when you're about 12.

FOR AGES 6-8

A Every girl and woman has a vagina, while all boys and men have a penis, like Daddy's. A vagina is a stretchy tube that starts between your legs and goes up into your body. Girls also have a clitoris, which is a little like a penis, but it is quite small, doesn't stick out much, and it's hard to see. A clitoris can get stiff like a penis, and when it does, it feels tingly and good. Sperm comes out through a man's penis, in semen. Girls don't do quite the same thing, but the vagina does produce some fluid to keep it smooth and comfortable, especially when a man and a woman have sexual intercourse. Girls have a small hole next to their clitoris for passing urine.

FOR AGES 8-11

A When a man and a woman, like Mom and Dad, want to have sexual intercourse, the vagina becomes moist and wet to make it easy for the penis to enter, and it feels very good. In fact, it is so enjoyable that both partners may have an orgasm. When a man has an orgasm, the semen with sperm in it spurts into the vagina: this is called an ejaculation. A woman doesn't ejaculate when she has an orgasm, but her vagina becomes more moist.

All penises get stiff and erect from time to time. Sometimes your clitoris probably gets hard, too, and you may want to touch it because it feels good. That's okay in private; it's normal and most girls and women do it. The vagina leads up into the womb or uterus, which is where a baby develops during pregnancy. The ovaries, which produce an egg every month, are well protected deep inside a woman's body, unlike a man's testicles, which hang outside his body so that they keep cool.

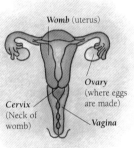

Womb (uterus)

Ovary (where eggs are made)

Cervix (Neck of womb)

Vagina

● *What is a period? p. 28* ● *What's masturbation? p. 32*

Q What's a penis?

● *Why do I have a penis?* ● *Why don't girls have a penis?*

● *Why does my penis get bigger/harder?* ● *What are testicles for?*

● *Why doesn't Daddy have breasts?* ● *What's a vagina?*

Like the questions about girls' anatomy, boys want to know about the things that are special to them. Most of these questions are from the boy's point of view, but girls will also want to be informed about boys to help them understand why boys and girls like and do different things. If possible, discuss the answers given here at the same time as "What's a vagina?" (p. 20) with your daughters and sons together so that each knows about the other.

WHAT'S BEHIND THIS QUESTION

None of these questions are prurient – in fact, they are intelligent. From the age of 2½, boys are very interested in the fact that they are boys, so they are curious about all their male features. They want to be like other boys and don't want to be mistaken for girls. By the age of about five, boys start comparing themselves to girls, mainly to find differences. Your son will also want to know if he and his father are made the same way – he loves identifying with his father. Later, when he either learns about or experiences a wet dream he'll want to be reassured that it is normal and if other boys and men he knows will have them, too – even Dad.

GUIDELINES FOR YOUR ANSWERS

● One of the best ways to reassure a boy that he is normal is to let him compare his penis with his father's, and to find out that it does the same things as his does.
● Four-year-old boys are intrigued by their genitals, because they have years of experience of this interesting part of them that squirts and tingles and that they can get hold of, but now they want to know more. This is normal; don't deter it. Be laid back, but also positive:

permit your young son's self-stimulation and sexual curiosity. Accept that your child is a sexual being who feels aroused through exploring his body. Never speak harshly to him about this; ignore it or distract him with another activity instead.
● Although children under five are interested in their genitals, and those of others, they in fact probably won't ask these questions because they usually take their anatomy for granted.

WHAT ELSE TO KNOW

● From birth to 18 months, it's normal for boys to experience penile erections and to touch and play with their penises. By the age of three, your toddler is still very interested in genitals, and in urine and feces.
● It's normal for six-year-olds to express concrete interest in sexuality by playing doctor, or "Mommies and Daddies." As long as it is safe, try to accept that this is not an erotic game as you would interpret it.
● Questions about the function of the penis lead naturally to questions about the vagina, from both boys and girls. Refer back to the questions and answers on pages 20 and 21, but remember that you never need to show a child a real vagina. Most children will accept that it is private. However, by seven or eight, you can show your child a simple drawing. In answer to a direct question from a nine- or ten-year-old boy, a father can explain what a vagina feels like to him.

Other things you may be asked...

■ *Why haven't I got a vagina?*

■ *Do all boys have the same kind of penis?*

■ *Does Daddy's penis get hard, too?*

■ *What happens inside my testicles?*

■ *What's a foreskin?*

■ *What's ejaculation?*

See also *What is sex? p. 18* ● *What's a vagina? p. 20* ● *What does "puberty" mean? p. 26* ● *What's masturbation? p. 32*

Children under four will rarely ask this question because they take their anatomy for granted. But if your child does begin to notice and ask about gender differences, base your answers on those given for the 4–6 age group below.

A All boys and men have penises. A penis does two things: it gets rid of water and other things that you don't need in your body in urine, and when a man is grown-up it helps him to make a baby. All penises grow hard now and then, especially if you touch or hold them. Daddy's penis is exactly like yours, except it's quite a bit bigger.

A Most of the time your penis is used to get rid of urine, but a penis can also become hard, so that when a man is grown up it can go easily into a woman's vagina to put sperm right inside, so a baby might be formed. A vagina is a stretchy tube that starts between a woman's legs and goes up inside her body. Your penis is very sensitive and it probably gets bigger sometimes without your being able to do anything about it – as if it was on automatic pilot – but it feels good. Girls and women don't have penises. They have a clitoris, which is small but also grows and tingles, a bit like a penis does. Near the clitoris is a small hole where urine comes out.

A An erection is the word for a penis that has become stiff. It is perfectly normal to have erections – it's part of growing up. By the time you're about 12 or so your testes will be making a lot of sperm day and night. When it has collected it just has to get out, so you might have a "wet dream," which just means that sperm comes out when you are asleep. That's normal and natural, and most boys have wet dreams.

Testes are sperm factories, and in order for sperm production to go smoothly the temperature of the testes must be lower than that of the rest of your body. That's why they hang outside the body in the scrotum. The foreskin is the circle of very flexible skin that protects the tip of your penis. The foreskin is sometimes removed when a boy is still a baby for religious reasons, and sometimes for medical reasons. It doesn't make any difference to the way the penis works.

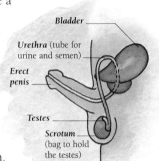

Bladder

Urethra (tube for urine and semen)

Erect penis

Testes

Scrotum (bag to hold the testes)

Q Why can't I take my clothes off?

● *Can I take a bath with you?* ● *Do I have to put my clothes on?*

● *Is it all right to walk around without my clothes on?*

● *Why do you and Daddy sometimes have no clothes on?*

The subject of nudity is unfortunately often surrounded by taboos, but there needn't be any inhibition within a family with children under 11. However, try to make young children aware that some people, particularly from an older generation such as grandparents, may see things differently, and that it is polite to respect their views and behave accordingly.

WHAT'S BEHIND THIS QUESTION

Up to the age of seven or eight, children are quite accepting of nudity in anyone. If they learn prudishness at all, they learn it from adults who are nervous about nakedness. To most children, nudity is quite normal and they may not understand why limits need to be set. However, even if you as a family are unconcerned about nudity, others – their own friends' parents just as much as members of an older generation – may not be. When they experience these differing viewpoints, your children are likely to question them.

GUIDELINES FOR YOUR ANSWERS

● Try not to program your children with your own hang-ups about nudity, if you have them. Your younger children will be naturally unembarrassed; take your lead from them.

● At around eight or nine, however, some children (particularly girls) may give you very clear signals that they are no longer comfortable about exposing their bodies. You may find that your daughter starts shutting her bedroom door or puts a "KEEP OUT" sign on it; she may want to lock the bathroom door for the first time and cover up when changing for swimming or sports practice. When this happens, respect her need for privacy. It is part and parcel of the beginnings of sexual awareness that precedes the onset of puberty. At the same time, try to help her maintain a positive attitude toward her appearance to avoid problems of self-esteem later.

● Try to be consistent about nudity. For instance, if you were in the habit of getting into the bathtub with your baby, it is not a very good idea just a year or two later to become coy about showing your body. You could not only confuse your child but also encourage furtiveness, secrecy, and loss of trust in you.

WHAT ELSE TO KNOW

● The fewer the limits set, the better. My own children followed me into the bathroom until they were five or six years old and felt free to come into the bathroom or bedroom anytime while I was dressing. Some parents may feel shy about this, but my primary concern was to make myself available to my children at all times, as well as making them feel comfortable with nudity and therefore with their own bodies.

● Of course, your child will also have to learn that outside your home, others may not be so open about nudity; you may need to explain that it's good manners to reduce someone else's embarrassment. What is perfectly acceptable at home may not be possible or advisable elsewhere – for instance, at someone's house or at the school carnival. Children understand these differences and will happily accommodate them – once you explain the reasons for them.

Other things you may be asked...

■ *Does it matter if boys and girls both have no clothes on?*

■ *Can I come into the bathroom with you?*

■ *Why does Grandma mind when I take my clothes off?*

■ *Why does Karen's Mommy say it's rude to have no clothes on?*

■ *Why does Karen get upset when I take my clothes off?*

See also *What's a vagina? p. 20* ● *What's a penis? p. 22* ● *What does "puberty" mean? p. 26*

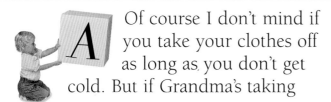

A Of course I don't mind if you take your clothes off as long as you don't get cold. But if Grandma's taking care of you and she'd prefer that you keep your clothes on, it's better to do as she wants – we don't want to hurt her feelings.

A I know it feels good to take your clothes off. Daddy and I often walk around without clothes on when we wake up. And you can come into the bathroom if you want to talk to me when I'm in there. But sometimes people are shy and it's not fair to make them feel uncomfortable, so get dressed for their sake.

A It's okay to play in cousin Lucy's backyard without clothes because Aunt Mary doesn't mind. But if you play at Karen's, it's better to keep your clothes on, because Karen is shy and her Mom doesn't like it. People from some places wear hardly any clothes at all, but others think it's better to cover their bodies, so when we're with other people we should respect their feelings about this. Daddy and I don't mind if you see us without clothes sometimes at home because we like our bodies, and it's nice not to have clothes covering them for a change.

A I do understand if you worry about someone seeing you when you're changing for swimming, and that you don't want your brother coming into the bathroom anymore when you're there. I remember feeling exactly the same myself at your age. It's part of growing up to begin to think you need more privacy. But remember he hasn't gotten to that stage yet. We could make a sign for your door saying "This is Jo's room!" or "KEEP OUT – PRIVATE." We'll put a lock on the bathroom door, too.

Q What does "puberty" mean?

- *Why does Michael's voice sound funny?* ● *What are hormones?*
- *When will I start to grow breasts?* ● *What's adolescence?*
- *Why is hair growing around my vagina/penis?*

When your child starts asking about puberty, take him seriously because this indicates that he is thinking about growing up. Children under six will rarely ask about puberty as such, but their questions might arise from seeing changes in older siblings or other young people close to your family.

WHAT'S BEHIND THIS QUESTION

This is one of the biggest and most challenging questions from a child, because he probably suspects it has something to do with sexuality. A younger child who actually includes the word "puberty" in a question will have heard the word used somewhere, but a child over six will know that all bodies change as they get older and will want to know about these changes.

GUIDELINES FOR YOUR ANSWERS

- Never dodge your child's questions about puberty.
- Find a good starting point by asking, "What particularly interests you about puberty?" or "Have you heard something about puberty already?"

- By the time your child is ten, you could include yourself by sharing your own experience of puberty.
- Never make fun of your child, and respect his need for privacy. This will encourage him to come to you when older to ask you more difficult questions, knowing you'll never criticize or judge.

WHAT ELSE TO KNOW

- A girl of nine or ten may begin to show early signs of puberty such as breast development and body hair, so she needs to know what to expect in good time.
- The best way to prepare your child for puberty is to give her accurate information on all aspects of the changes that happen to boys and girls, including menstruation, fertility, wet dreams, and masturbation.

Other things you may be asked...

- *When did you start/finish puberty ?*
- *What does "fertile" mean?*
- *When did you start to shave?*

 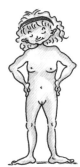 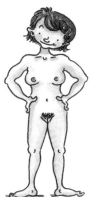  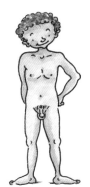 

At age 6–7
girls are flat-chested and hairless. They lose rounded baby tummies but have no "waistline."

At age 10–11
many girls will be showing breast development and pubic hair begins to grow.

By age 14–15
girls' bodies will be rounded, breasts enlarged, and body hair will have grown.

By age 15–17
boys' shoulders will have broadened, the genitals enlarged, and facial hair appeared.

At age 12–14
boys' voices begin to break, and body hair starts around the genitals and underarms.

At age 6–7
boys' bodies are like girls' in shape, and the penis and testes are small and hairless.

See also *Where did I come from? p. 12* ● *What is sex? p. 18* ● *What is a period? p. 28* ● *What's masturbation? p. 32*

Children under the age of four will rarely ask this question unless they hear the word used by other people. If a mature 3½-year-old child raises the subject, base your answers on those provided for the 4–6 age group, below.

A Puberty is a time when lots of very exciting things change in your body and you really begin to grow up. It's when girls start to grow breasts and boys' voices get deeper, and boys and girls sometimes get pimples, but it won't happen to you until you're older.

A Puberty is the time during your teens when you grow taller and your body begins to change shape. Girls grow breasts, and boys' shoulders get broader and more muscular. Girls start their monthly periods, which show their bodies are getting ready to have a baby when they are older, and they grow hair under their arms and around their vaginas. Boys start making sperm in their testes and grow hair around their penises and testes, under their arms and on their chest, legs, and face as well, so eventually they have to start shaving. Their voices get much lower, too, like mine/Dad's.

A At puberty your body starts to grow really fast, inside and out. Girls usually start to change a couple of years before boys. In girls, special chemicals called hormones, produced by the ovaries, help change girls' shape so their waists get smaller, their breasts grow, their hips and thighs get rounder, and they start their monthly periods, usually around the age of 12 or 13. From then on a girl is fertile – her body is getting ready to grow a baby when she's older.

In boys, hormones produced in the testes make their muscles develop and their shoulders get broader, and they have erections and wet dreams. The penis and scrotum get bigger, and these are all signs that they are beginning to produce sperm and be fertile, too – able to father children. Boys' voices gradually get deeper – or break – when they are about 13 or 14, and they may need to start shaving when they're about 16. Both boys and girls grow hair between their legs and under their arms, and they may get pimples. Everyone produces more sweat, so it's a good idea to bathe or shower more frequently. The time when these changes happen is called "adolescence." During adolescence, it's normal for boys and girls to feel a little moody – it isn't surprising when you think about all the important and exciting things that are happening at the same time!

For boys: "I might start shaving when I'm about 16, and my voice might break when I'm 14, like Dad."

For girls: "I might need my first bra when I'm 12, like Mom did."

Q What is a period?

- *Why are you/is Mommy bleeding?* ● *Why don't boys have periods?*
- *Do periods last a long time?* ● *When will I start my periods?*
- *What's menstruation?* ● *Will I ever stop having periods?*

Menstruation questions need to be handled sensitively but positively. Young children may equate bleeding with pain and injury so they need to be reassured that it is normal. Older girls and boys both need to be prepared for this natural change in girls' bodies, but girls need more detail than boys.

WHAT'S BEHIND THIS QUESTION

Periods could start to be part of children's conversation around the age of seven, although a younger child might hear the word much earlier. I remember my four-year-old son asking me what "temperstation" was, after he heard me telling my husband I was menstruating. Children often approach the subject furtively, as though it were something dirty and distasteful, because many adults can be secretive about menstruation, treating it like a taboo. For this reason you may find that questions about it are somewhat challenging.

It is important to be open with your child from her first question, no matter how young she is. Children are quick to pick up signs of unwillingness to talk and will take advantage of this if you aren't candid. The subject may arise if a younger child finds tampons or sanitary napkins in the bathroom or notices bloodstains on underwear, especially if you allow your child into the bathroom with you. Seeing menstrual blood can be quite alarming to a young child, who may associate it with an injury and might think Mommy has hurt herself or is ill, so it is essential to give her immediate reassurance that everything is natural and normal.

GUIDELINES FOR YOUR ANSWERS

- Girls need to be aware that it is perfectly normal for periods to start anywhere between about age 10 and 15.
- Girls should be reassured that the blood may be brown rather than red to start with, that early periods may not be regular, and that there may be abdominal pain, which is easily treated with pain medication.
- Try to emphasize to boys that they should be sympathetic to girls and women who are menstruating; explain that periods can be painful and may make girls and women a little moody.
- Avoid negative connotations – don't say "That's when I'm crabby" or refer to menstruation as "the curse." Make sure children know that life goes on as normal.

WHAT ELSE TO KNOW

- Girls who begin to menstruate without being forewarned – and many still do – can react badly. They may suffer profound shock, think they're ill or, worse, dying, then may grow up to feel ambivalent about their sexuality and have difficulty with relationships.
- Help your daughter by telling her in good time – a likely start date is the age that you (her mother) began.
- When your daughter is about ten, explain to her how sanitary napkins and tampons are used.

Other things you may be asked...

- *Does everyone know when you're having your period?*
- *How do you stop the bleeding?*
- *Do periods hurt?*
- *What's a tampon for?*
- *Can I take gym when I have my period?*

Maxi pad
Best when periods become regular.

Tampon
The simplest internal "napkin" for active teenage girls and women.

Tampon with applicator
Many teenage girls prefer to start with this type of tampon.

Mini pad
Slim, fitted napkin is good for scanty periods.

See also *Where did I come from? p. 12* ● *What's a vagina? p. 20* ● *What does "puberty" mean? p. 26*

A A period is the time every month when Mommy's body reminds her she can have another baby if she wants to. Don't worry, Mommy's not ill and she hasn't hurt herself.

A A period and menstruation are just different words for the same thing – it's the time every 28 days or so that most women's bodies show that they're able to have a baby – that they're fertile. Girls normally start having periods when they are about 12 or 13, at the time of their lives that's called puberty, when lots of changes happen to their bodies to get them ready for having a baby one day. During her period a girl bleeds through her vagina for a few days every month – but it's quite normal; it happens to most girls and women every month, except when they're going to have a baby. During her period, a woman wears a sanitary napkin inside her pants. Most girls start with these; later they might wear a "napkin" inside, called a tampon. Their Mommies show them how to use it.

A Getting a period or menstruating means that every month the hormones from a girl's ovaries get her body ready to become pregnant, though of course most of the time she doesn't. Most girls don't choose to become pregnant until they're grown-up enough to take care of the baby. One of these hormones is called estrogen, and it makes the lining of the womb thick and healthy in preparation for a baby. If a woman doesn't get pregnant, the uterus no longer needs to be ready to grow a baby, so the lining just comes away and it bleeds. When the bleeding stops the whole cycle starts again. Boys and men don't get periods because they don't have a uterus.

Nobody else knows when a girl has her period; she can do everything she does normally, including sports – even swimming if she's wearing a tampon. Sanitary napkins and tampons are comfortable and don't get in the way. You just have to remember to change them often. Some girls get cramps during periods but the pain doesn't usually last long. Women stop having periods when they're about 50 because the hormones that control the menstrual cycle stop being produced.

Q What's a contraceptive?

- *Why don't you get pregnant every time you have sex?*

- *How do you stop having a baby?* • *What's the Pill?*

- *What's a condom/rubber?* • *What's safe sex?*

Contraception questions are unlikely to come from children under six, but once your child starts going to school there could well be an older child who thinks it's funny to produce a condom in the schoolyard for a joke. It is important to be open, as your child needs accurate information about contraception before he is likely to be sexually active. Knowledge of contraception encourages responsible sexual conduct.

- Although younger children are unlikely to raise this subject in the form of the questions given above, it may arise naturally in the course of other conversations, for instance, about where babies come from.
- Don't shy away from questions about contraception or make the mistake of thinking it encourages sexual activity. It does the opposite.
- Where possible, show your child the different types of contraceptive and how they work – the drawings below will help, but it's even better to show them the real thing, or promise to do it later, and keep your promise.

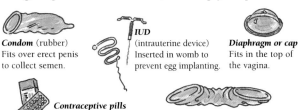

Condom (rubber)
Fits over erect penis
to collect semen.

IUD
(intrauterine device)
Inserted in womb to
prevent egg implanting.

Diaphragm or cap
Fits in the top of
the vagina.

Contraceptive pills
Hormones which
prevent ovulation.

Femidom – female condom
Fits inside the vagina.

——— WHAT'S BEHIND THIS QUESTION ———

If your child asks questions about contraception, she probably knows quite a bit about sex already. Some of it may be accurate but most will have been acquired as half-truths in the schoolyard – almost certainly exaggerated, and undoubtedly mystifying. In any event, to understand contraception a child needs to know the basics of sex and reproduction, so make sure she has that understanding first, by asking detailed questions, like "where did you first hear about contraception?" or "what kind of contraceptives are you thinking about?" If the questions are about specific types of contraceptives, ask specific questions, like "Have you seen a rubber?" "Was someone talking about condoms today?" or "How did you hear about safe sex?" This will help both to guide you to the source of the query and give you an idea of your child's present level of knowledge.

——— GUIDELINES FOR YOUR ANSWERS ———

- There's no specific age when children should have information about contraception – it depends on your child. You may have to give explanations earlier to a sexually aware daughter than to a shy son – or vice versa.

——— WHAT ELSE TO KNOW ———

- There is no reason why you should not demonstrate how a condom works to children over eight – boys *and* girls – by putting it over a banana. Make a game of it – blow it up like a balloon. It's a sure way of demystifying something that often becomes a focus for uninformed discussion about sex among children.
- A discussion of contraception needs to include the unwelcome outcomes of sex: unwanted pregnancy, AIDS, herpes, and other sexually transmitted diseases.

Other things you may be asked...

- *How do contraceptives work?*
- *How do you put on a condom?*
- *Is there a rubber for girls?*
- *Where do you get contraceptives?*
- *What happens if you don't take your pills?*

See also *Where did I come from? p. 12* • *What is sex? p. 18* • *What's a vagina? p. 20* • *What's a penis? p. 22*

A People who love each other, like Mommy and Daddy, use contraceptives to stop them from making a baby until they think they are really ready to have one.

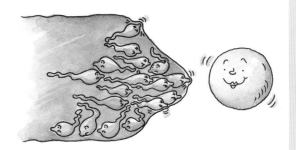

FOR AGES 2–6

A Using a contraceptive prevents pregnancy. There are lots of kinds of contraceptives, some for women and some for men, which work in different ways. The types of contraceptive which are used most often are the Pill and the condom. A woman can take birth control pills every day; she gets them from the doctor. The pills stop eggs being released from the woman's ovaries. If she stops taking the pills, she could grow a baby the next month, so a couple must always use another sort of contraceptive when a woman stops taking the Pill, unless they want a baby. A man can wear a condom, which he puts on his penis when it is stiff. It catches the sperm so they don't go inside the woman's body. Condoms also stop people from passing diseases from one to another when they have sex. When a man uses a condom the man and woman are both safe from catching bad illnesses like AIDS.

FOR AGES 6–8

A Contraceptives prevent pregnancies, which is why any man and woman who are having sex MUST use a contraceptive if they don't want a baby. Nothing else will do. When a couple has sex they share responsibility for contraception. Usually, they decide together what to use. A woman can take a contraceptive pill every day, or she can have an IUD (intrauterine device) put inside her womb by a doctor to prevent pregnancy. She could also wear a rubber disc, called a cervical cap or diaphragm, which fits inside her vagina to keep the sperm out of the womb. A man can wear a condom, which stops sperm from going into a woman's body. Wearing condoms is part of practicing "safe sex," which means having sex in ways that stop certain diseases being passed on. There are also condoms for women, which fit up inside the vagina, instead of just at the top, like a cap. Lots of different stores sell condoms, but other contraceptives come from a doctor or a special place called a family planning clinic. But Mom and Dad are ready to talk to you about contraception whenever you want to.

FOR AGES 8–11

● *What is a period? p. 28* ● *What is AIDS? p. 92*

Q What's masturbation?

- *Can I touch myself down there?* • *Do you masturbate?*

- *Is it dirty to touch myself down there?*

- *What does "playing with yourself" mean?*

Masturbation is one of the most difficult questions for many parents to face – not because the subject is in itself complicated but because of their own attitudes about it. Your child has the right to be relaxed about masturbation. Being clear in your own mind that masturbation is normal and beneficial will help to dispel the myths that surround it.

───── WHAT'S BEHIND THIS QUESTION ─────

Your child may well start hearing the word at school and begin to wonder what it means. She may also have heard from other children all sorts of myths about masturbation being dirty and having dreadful consequences. Most of these myths originate from anxious adults who can't cope with the idea of young children stimulating themselves sexually. So your child's questions about masturbation, or about "touching" or "rubbing," probably arise because someone has scolded them or remarked on it.

───── GUIDELINES FOR YOUR ANSWERS ─────

- This is a difficult question for many parents because of misunderstandings starting in their own childhood. Masturbation is not bad in itself; treat it as a normal part of growing up, and don't plant the seeds of shame.
- Tolerate or ignore masturbation; if questions arise answer them simply and factually; agree that "it feels good to touch your penis," but set limits: "This is something we do in private." If your child absent-mindedly masturbates in public, treat it as you would bad manners or thoughtlessness: "Those people would be more comfortable if you didn't do that here."

- Up to the age of five, one child touching another is nearly always innocent. Make sure that one child is not an unwilling victim and that he or she is not trying to put things into him/herself. The exception to this would be a child who has been abused when very young.
- If a child talks about someone who is significantly older and more developed touching her, you should treat this as a danger signal. Calmly ascertain exactly what has happened (if anything) and be vigilant when she's in the company of that person in the future.

───── WHAT ELSE TO KNOW ─────

- It is important to remember that all babies explore their genitals from about four months. This is a continuous process of development and children never naturally stop touching or feeling themselves. As they get older they may realize that touching their genitals is pleasurable, but a young child's masturbation has nothing to do with sex as we think of it; it stems from a desire to explore and understand.
- Since it's normal for children to touch their genitals, don't be surprised if your child reacts defensively to any suggestion that it is "dirty" or "harmful." It isn't – masturbation is only harmful if you react negatively to it.
- Masturbation is a healthy and natural way to release tension. The only time I would be concerned is if a child was masturbating habitually to escape from a horrible world because he was being emotionally deprived. A child like this needs help; the way to correct it is to give love, not punishment.

Other things you may be asked...

- *Does it matter if Susan touches my penis?*
- *Can Richard touch me down there, too?*
- *Is masturbation bad for you?*
- *Does everyone masturbate?*
- *Why does my penis stick up when I hold it?*

See also *What is sex? p. 18* • *Does sex feel good? p. 34* • *Why can't I talk to strangers? p. 76*

Children under the age of four will rarely ask this question because exploring their bodies is normal and unremarkable. If a mature 3½-year-old raises the subject in any way, base your answers on the 4–6 age group, which are given below.

A It doesn't matter if you touch yourself there, but it's best to do it at home, where it's private. **Boys**: Susan's only four so it doesn't matter if she touches your penis, but ask her not to.
Girls: Since little Sam is only three, it's okay, but tell him not to. It's private. He mustn't try to touch you inside – you must tell me if he does.

A It doesn't matter if you touch yourself down there. Most people do, boys and girls and grown-ups, because it feels good. A few people may say it's wrong – it isn't at all, but we usually do it in private. The big word for it is "masturbation," and it's so normal that everyone does it sometimes.

A Masturbation means touching or rubbing the clitoris in girls or the penis in boys – and it's perfectly normal. It feels good and most people do it – grown-ups, too. It's never bad for you and nothing terrible will happen to you if you do it, but it's best to do it in private. You won't go deaf or blind or get pimples or grow hair on the palms of your hands – and you can tell whoever told you those things that they are just silly stories and they simply aren't true.

Sometimes a boy's penis or a girl's clitoris just seem to get hard and to tingle for no reason at all, and it's a normal reaction to want to rub it, which can feel very good. But if you don't want to touch yourself down there, that's okay, too.

When boys and girls get to be a little older, they may have an orgasm from masturbating. When an older boy has an orgasm he ejaculates and semen comes out of the penis. An orgasm is a very exciting feeling that spreads over your whole body; afterward you may feel a little sleepy.

Q Does sex feel good?

- *What is ejaculation?* • *What's an orgasm?* • *What's oral sex?*
- *Do you have an orgasm every time ?* • *Do girls ejaculate?*
- *Does everyone have orgasms?* • *What's "coming"?*

As children get older and more knowing, they will begin to ask more searching questions, especially if they hear slang words used about sex among their friends. Answering these questions frankly and accurately could be difficult for you because of your sensibilities and feelings about privacy, but for your children's sake try to deal with them coolly.

WHAT'S BEHIND THIS QUESTION

I feel that these questions are mainly the province of the older age groups. Accept that your child is quite worldly by the time he starts looking for answers to questions like these. He is really searching for good, solid, accurate information. Any child who asks these questions can deal with detailed explanations of sexual intercourse – in fact, the questions may well arise out of conversations you've already had about sex, and your child is showing his trust in you if he brings you additional questions about sex.

GUIDELINES FOR YOUR ANSWERS

- Don't cop out. You're letting your child down if you use an excuse like "I don't know how to describe it – I can't find the words." The truth of the matter is you don't have to. Just keep it simple.
- Although older children are the ones most likely to raise these issues, a child under six may hear a word like "orgasm" spoken and could ask what it means. As with other questions about sexuality, you need to provide only the simplest explanation.
- Even your knowing 11-year-old may be a little frightened by some of the information, so watch closely for signs of anxiety and reassure him that he'll find out

that it's normal and natural when it finally happens to him – but that it won't be for a long time yet.
- Be simple and nonjudgmental, and tonelessly factual, like describing the weather. Check that you're on the right track by saying, "Is this the sort of thing you want to know?" so that you don't blunder on unnecessarily.

WHAT ELSE TO KNOW

- I would have felt delinquent if I hadn't given you some help in how to answer this and related questions. "What is 69?" is only included to cover all eventualities. If you're uncomfortable, don't discuss such subjects spontaneously, but if your child faces you with them, use these answers to help you. You'll never need to use all the information here – pick and choose what's appropriate at the time.
- Giving this information simply and straightforwardly in the way I have described is not salacious. It is preparing your child to manage the choppy waters of puberty. More and better information gives them the best chance. Children who are given information about sex by their own parents are better able to act responsibly in the future. They will have the strength to stand their ground, say no (and to more than sex, too), so respect your child's needs and try wherever possible to stress that enjoyment of sex should be mutual between two people when each one has the responsibility for the other's pleasure. People mustn't be used.

Other things you may be asked...

- *What's a blow job?*
- *What's mutual masturbation?*
- *What does 69 mean?*
- *Do boys/girls have orgasms?*
- *What's anal sex?*
- *Do men do oral sex with women, too?*

See also *What is sex? p. 18* • *What's masturbation? p. 32* • *What is AIDS? p. 92*

Children under six are very unlikely to ask this question. If they do hear the word and ask its meaning, simply say:

"An orgasm's a good feeling that starts deep inside your body. You'll find out more about it when you get older."

A An orgasm is a very good feeling that people get after they have been rubbing or touching their clitoris or penis. You probably won't have this feeling until you're quite a bit older – say, 13 or 14. Men and women have this feeling as part of sexual intercourse when they feel especially loving toward each other. But it doesn't happen to people this way until they're grown up – at least 17 or 18.

There are some slang words that mean having an orgasm, but they're sometimes used to make people feel bad, so it's best not to say them.

A During an orgasm a girl feels intense pleasure in her clitoris and vagina, and a boy feels it in his penis. From the age of about 13, boys and girls can give themselves orgasms by masturbating. An orgasm is usually the climax of sexual intercourse, but grown-ups can also give each other orgasms by masturbating each other or by licking or sucking the clitoris or penis. If they do it at the same time it's called "69" because they lie head to toe. Boys and men find it much easier to have orgasms when they're enjoying sexual intercourse – it happens nearly every time, but it may not for girls and women. If a couple doesn't want to have a baby, having oral sex or masturbating each other means sperm don't go inside the vagina so the woman can't get pregnant (but AIDS can still be transmitted). Two women can do these things to each other and so can two men. Anal sex is when the penis goes into the anus. It can happen between two men or a man and a woman, as long as they are happy about it. With any kind of sex, people have to think of each other and be gentle.

Q What does it mean if you're "gay"?

- *What is a homosexual?* ● *What is a lesbian?*
- *How can you tell if someone is gay?*
- *Why are some people gay?* ● *Will I be a homosexual?*

Children have no difficulty in accepting a variety of relationships among the adults they know, but they will be curious about the differences. Giving straightforward answers to questions about homosexual relationships, just as you would about heterosexual ones, will help prevent prejudice or misunderstanding from taking hold in your child.

different from anyone else, and to say that they are different is the same as saying that anyone of a different race, skin color, or religious background to you is somehow inferior. You can emphasize that these should never be grounds for cruel treatment or bullying.

● Preschool children will probably not ask about homosexuality or what "gay" means because even if they hear the words, they are unlikely to be sensitive to the context in which the word was used.

● There is no need to go into detail about male homosexual practices with children under eight years old, who have enough difficulty understanding the mechanics of heterosexual sex and reproduction. But when discussing homosexual relationships, remember to put the same emphasis on love, respect, and emotions as you would in any discussion about sex.

WHAT ELSE TO KNOW

We have no way of knowing who will be homosexual (loving the same gender as oneself) or heterosexual (loving the opposite gender), and one of your children could easily turn out to be homosexual. If you yourself judge gay people to be abnormal, your child will be afraid to come to you ever again with sensitive subjects, particularly if she turns out to have homosexual preferences from an early age, as many homosexuals have said they do. Your child may get into all sorts of trouble because she has lost confidence in you, and will try to deal with problems without your help. You will in effect be instrumental in losing your child.

WHAT'S BEHIND THIS QUESTION

There's probably nothing out of the way behind questions of this sort. Your child is fact-finding, just as if she were asking, what's an optician? an accountant? a sprinter? Do find out, however, if your child has heard the word used in a pejorative way or in a joke. This is almost certainly the case if your child asks you the meaning of one of the slang words for a homosexual, and you'll have to correct the prejudice that your child has unwittingly acquired.

GUIDELINES FOR YOUR ANSWERS

● Ask your child where she first came across the word, because this is an excellent opportunity to teach your child tolerance. You can say that homosexuals are no

Other things you may be asked...

- ■ *Are they born like that?*
- ■ *Do gay people have sex?*
- ■ *Do gay people get married?*
- ■ *Can gay people have children?*
- ■ *Are some women gay?*

See also *What is sex? p. 18* ● *What's a contraceptive? p. 30* ● *What is AIDS? p. 92*

Children under age six are unlikely to ask questions about homosexuality because close friendships between the same sex are not noteworthy, and they are not aware of different adults' sexual orientation. If a mature 5–6-year-old raises the subject, adapt my answer for the 6–8 age group.

FOR AGES 2–6

A gay person likes people of the same gender, so a gay man is attracted to men and a gay woman – a lesbian – prefers other women, and they can have sex together if they love each other. "Gay" is another way of describing someone who is homosexual, which is the word for someone who falls in love with other people of the same sex, or gender. The "homo" part of the word homosexual means "the same." People who fall in love with someone of the opposite sex are called heterosexuals, because the "hetero" part of the word comes from the Greek word for "different." There are lots of slang words that people use for male homosexuals, but they aren't good words to use. There aren't as many slang words for lesbians. Loving someone of the same gender is no different from loving someone of the opposite gender. It's all love. Everyone needs that.

FOR AGES 6–8

We don't yet know why some people are homosexual and some aren't. Two homosexual women (lesbians) or two gay men can have sex together if they love each other. Gay men make love by kissing and cuddling and masturbating each other by touching each other's penises, or one putting his penis in the other man's anus. Lesbians kiss and cuddle and masturbate each other. They can't usually have children of their own, but some lesbian women do have babies with a heterosexual man as the father.

Some people like both men and women (they're called bisexual) and can become parents by having a relationship with the opposite sex. I don't know if you'll be gay or not, but it wouldn't matter if you were, I'll love you just the same. Gay people need their families and friends to be kind and loving to them just like anyone else. Some people who are ignorant think they're bad and will call them names. They're wrong, and you shouldn't use cruel or insulting words.

FOR AGES 8–11

QUESTIONS ABOUT

What are ghosts?

Are any spirits kind?

What does dead mean?

When will I die?

Is God a man or a woman?

Why do some unborn babies die?

DEATH AND BEREAVEMENT ● MISCARRIAGE ● STILLBIRTH ●

THE UNKNOWN

Questions about difficult subjects like death or the existence of God pose a dilemma for parents, particularly if you do not yourselves hold firm religious beliefs. Try not to steer away from these subjects when they come up. If you

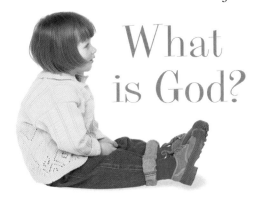

What is God?

are a believer, your own faith will obviously be reflected in your answers. But there are other points of view which your children will experience – so it is important to try to foster tolerance and the right of others to hold different views. On the whole it is more worrying for your child if you sidestep questions about the existence of ghosts or monsters, because their imaginations will start working overtime instead, and provide them with fanciful explanations that are more frightening than the truth. It is far better to be as honest and factual as possible, while at the same time being sensitive to your children's fears. Remember that their questions about the unknown are never frivolous, so don't laugh at them or make light of them in any way. Take them seriously but don't dwell on them. Answer questions and worries immediately, and then try to steer your child toward a more positive train of thought or another activity.

Where does God live?

RELIGION ● THE EXISTENCE OF GOD ● IRRATIONAL FEARS ●

Q What happens when you die?

- *Why do people and animals die?* ● *What does "dead" mean?*
- *Do I have to die?* ● *Where do people go when they die?*
- *How do you know if someone's dead?* ● *When will I die?*

Most children are sensitive about the subject of death, if only because we often talk of it in hushed tones. But secrecy can lead to confusion and anxiety. It is not helpful either to your children or you as parents to avoid the subject. Dealing with questions as best you can is a way of helping the whole family cope with a bereavement.

WHAT'S BEHIND THIS QUESTION

Young children can't conceive that life can end; even a hint of this eventuality not only stimulates a rush of questions, mainly about themselves and the ones they turn to for love and care, but also terror lest their own lives end or they find themselves without one of their family. Children often count anyone they see regularly as family, not just their relatives. I remember my three- and five-year-olds listing their "family" as: "Mom, Dad, Grandma, Grandpa, you, me, Ollie and Barney (brothers), Hazie (aunt), Oona and Slater (cousins who visited weekly), Frank (uncle who lived with us), Mary (cleaner), Alfie and Beaux (dogs), Cinnamon (cat), Alain (gardener), Jacky (secretary), Bob (laundryman)," and so on. A child could be concerned and anxious if anyone in his or her extended "family" were ill or injured.

GUIDELINES FOR YOUR ANSWERS

● You should try to be clear about the subject of death right from the start. Never use euphemisms such as "Grandma has just gone to sleep." It could make your child afraid of going to sleep, and you'll witness troublesome bedtimes and nightmares. Neither should you say, "Grandpa's gone away." Your child will lose her trust in you when Grandpa doesn't come back.
● Use religious explanations depending on your beliefs, but be prepared for childhood logic like "If God loves us why did he let our baby die?"

● Be truthful, but try to keep your own emotions in check because you may frighten your child. This doesn't mean that you should not share your grief if you are particularly upset by a bereavement. Let your child know why you are sad – explain that you miss the person who has died very much, but stress the positive memories you have of that person.
● Use examples from a child's experience to explain death. For instance, talk about a baby bird that has died because it fell out of a nest, or the death of a pet, or even leaves dying in autumn. This is a way of showing that all things die, and that it's natural. Check that your child understands and repeat if necessary.
● If a pet dies, most preschool children will simply be curious to find out what has happened to the animal and a short answer will be enough.

WHAT ELSE TO KNOW

Your child may not be able to cope with philosophy or faith, so keep it very simple when you portray death in religious terms or she will be more mystified than ever. Don't portray death as painful because that's very frightening to your child.

Other things you may be asked...

- *Did he die because he'd been bad?*
- *What's a funeral/cremation?*
- *What happens to them in the coffin?*
- *Do people wake up after they've died?*
- *What will I do if you die?*

See also *Why do some babies die? p. 42* ● *What is God? p. 44* ● *What is AIDS? p. 92*

A "Dead" means a person or animal stops breathing and their body doesn't work anymore. Usually people and animals only die when they have grown very old.

A Something that dies – like that dead baby bird we saw last summer – can't come back. Most people and animals don't know when they're dying. Their heart stops or they quietly stop breathing.

A Nobody really knows exactly what happens when we die, but our bodies stop working: we stop breathing, the heart doesn't beat, the muscles don't work, and the brain stops thinking. Dying is final; the whole body just stops. Most people die naturally because they're very old and their bodies are worn out. Usually they don't feel pain and just gradually become unconscious and gently die. But some people die from serious illnesses or accidents. No one knows for sure where people go after they die, but we know there's no more worry or pain and that's good. You and I are so healthy that we probably won't die until we're much, much older.

A You will die one day, everybody does, but it's such a long way off that you don't need to think about it. But dying is natural, and although we're sad to lose someone we love very much, we must be prepared for older people like Grandma and Grandpa to die one day. We won't forget them and all the good things we did together. When people die, their bodies are put into a wooden box called a coffin which may be buried in a grave. No one wakes up in a coffin because a doctor checks that a person really is dead before he or she is put in it. Other people are cremated – burned – after they die, and their ashes are kept at the crematorium or spread on the ground somewhere they used to be very happy. A funeral is a chance to honor the life of someone who died. People can say a final goodbye and share their good memories of when the person was alive.

Q Why do some babies die?

- *What is a miscarriage?* • *What is a stillbirth?*
- *What's an abortion?* • *If you fall down, will the baby die?*
- *Is it worse for the baby to die before or after it's born?*

The loss of a baby through miscarriage or stillbirth is a tragedy, particularly for the mother, but it can be difficult for other children in the family to understand the grief felt for an entity they haven't had time to get to know. Giving factual answers to your children's questions can allay their fears and help them cope with grief.

WHAT'S BEHIND THIS QUESTION

Children of all ages are interested in what happened to them when they were babies, even in events long before they were born. They're also interested in what could have happened to them when they were younger. Your child probably won't ask this question unless he has heard about a miscarriage or stillbirth. If you have told your child that you are expecting another baby, or if you or someone close has the misfortune to have experienced a miscarriage, stillbirth, or prematurity, the questions will stem from feelings of anxiety about the same thing happening again. Older children may have heard something about abortion, and the question should be answered honestly.

GUIDELINES FOR YOUR ANSWERS

- Take your child's questions seriously but be reassuring – he is probably frightened. You might ask, "Are you afraid of anything?" before you start.
- Your child will need lots of encouragement to believe that stillbirth and neonatal death are so rare that it isn't necessary to worry about them.
- It is also helpful to tell children that babies who miscarry are often "weak" and that they probably wouldn't have lived for very long anyway.

- If you have had a miscarriage, emphasize that what you want is another wonderful, healthy child like him, and that one miss doesn't mean any future pregnancy will also end in miscarriage.
- Use any experience of death among family or close friends which your child may already have had to explain that you can say goodbye to an unborn baby lost in a late miscarriage or stillbirth in the same positive way.

WHAT ELSE TO KNOW

Some statistics might help you as background to your answers. It is said that a third of all first pregnancies end in the first eight weeks, and many women do not even realize they are pregnant when it happens. There are two main reasons for early miscarriage:

- The first is that the fetus is abnormal in some way and that it's nature's way of dealing with seriously damaged offspring.
- The second is that the uterus is in some way immature and wouldn't be strong enough to carry the baby to term – it needs a "trial run" before it's ready.

Other things you may be asked...

- *Do babies ever die in their Mommies' tummies?*
- *Will you die if the baby dies?*
- *Does it hurt the baby when it dies?*
- *How does the baby get out if it's dead?*
- *How do you know the baby's dead?*

See also *Where did I come from? p. 12* • *How does the baby grow inside you? p. 14* • *How does the baby get out? p. 16*

A Some babies are too weak to grow properly, so they don't get born. It doesn't happen very often – most babies grow up big and strong like you.

A Some unborn babies never grow properly and die when they're tiny, then slip out through their Mommies' vaginas. Sometimes a baby dies just after it's born, especially if it is born before it's ready. The baby's Mommy is all right, although she'll be very sad.

A "miscarriage" means that for some reason a baby dies in its Mommy's tummy and the pregnancy ends long before the baby is ready to be born. It's very rare for a baby to die after it's born unless it has something really wrong with its heart or lungs or blood, or it was born much too early. It's better for a Mommy and baby if the unborn baby dies when it is still very tiny. Then the Mommy may not even feel when it happens. But if it's bigger, a mother nearly always knows because the baby stops kicking. Our baby is still kicking – feel it! Healthy babies like you were are so firmly attached that nothing will move them until they're ready to be born – not even falling down the stairs!

A When unborn babies die it is usually because they aren't properly formed. If they are seriously abnormal – missing the heart or the brain – they die very soon, usually during the first three months of pregnancy.

If a baby dies later on during pregnancy, it may be because the placenta, which helps to feed the baby and give it oxygen, isn't working very well or because the mother is very ill. When a baby dies in pregnancy and the mother loses it, it's called a "spontaneous abortion," which means it happens by itself. If for some reason a pregnancy has to be stopped by doctors it is also called an abortion. People usually use the word "miscarriage" for a baby that dies from natural causes, and the word "abortion" for a pregnancy that is stopped on purpose. An early miscarriage doesn't cause pain to the baby and not usually to the mother; the tiny baby slips out like a menstrual period. But when the baby is more than 3in (7cm) long it is visible, and the parents are very upset.

If a baby who grows through pregnancy dies just before or at the birth, it is called a "still-birth." The baby probably doesn't feel pain. A stillbirth is sad; the baby is named and there is a funeral and people grieve for the baby like we did when Grandpa died. But stillbirths are rare: they happen only if something is really wrong.

● *What happens when you die? p. 40*

Q What is God?

● *Who is God?* ● *Is God a man or a woman?*

● *Do you believe in God?* ● *Where does God live?*

● *Did God make the world/me?* ● *Is God black or white?*

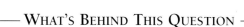

Whether or not you as parents are believers, at some stage your child is likely to ask pointed and searching questions about the nature of God. It is a good idea to think through for yourself what your answers will be. Children can be surprisingly profound in their thinking because they come to subjects like this with open minds.

—— WHAT'S BEHIND THIS QUESTION ——

These are the kinds of questions a child being brought up in a basically Judeo-Christian background might ask, whether or not you as a family practice a particular religion. In most Western countries with a Judeo-Christian historical tradition the whole culture is permeated with imagery that children will notice, including the idea of a single all-powerful being called "God." Your young child won't be asking questions about faith – it's a concept most children can't grasp till the age of seven or eight, when they begin to understand other complicated concepts like justice, charity, and equality. But almost all children are fascinated by superhuman beings who appear to be all-knowing and all-seeing. Their questions often relate to the extent of God's omnipotence and omnipresence (they may hear someone say that "God is everywhere" or that "God knows what you are doing all the time"), so they're looking for boundaries.

—— GUIDELINES FOR YOUR ANSWERS ——

● Humanizing God (as opposed to Jesus) is not necessarily a good idea because it can lead to intolerance of other religions' concepts of God. The idea of God is a difficult one to explain simply and in an unbiased way.

● If you're a believer, you naturally want your child to think the way that you do and vice versa if you are a nonbeliever. Faith in something is essential for most people's happiness and equilibrium, but try not to be too hard on your child if she has doubts or lacks enthusiasm. As your children get older, help them make their own minds up about it. If they see religion as something inflexible and intolerant, it could make them hostile to you and eventually may lead them to reject all faith – including faith in you.

● A healthy spiritual life is something all children can benefit from, as long as it is not used blindly to justify political or even military actions.

● Teach your child that people who believe in God generally see God as a force for good and love. Most religions acknowledge that human beings are imperfect; in fact, many religions are based on a human need to attain some sort of perfection through God. Where you can, relate faith – yours or other people's – to the world we live in and the reality of people's behavior.

—— WHAT ELSE TO KNOW ——

● You will probably want to answer these questions according to your own beliefs. However, although I have written some from a Christian standpoint, I have also tried to show the range of beliefs about the nature of God from a non-Christian perspective.

● Even if you're a nonbeliever you still need to explain what is meant by "God." Remember your children will eventually make up their own minds about spirituality, and you should encourage them to do so.

Other things you may be asked...

■ *What's a worshiper?*

■ *What's a believer?*

■ *Why does God let people die?*

■ *Why do my friends have different gods from me?*

See also *What happens when you die? p. 40* ● *What is religion? p. 46*

A God is love. When I say, "I love you," that's God. God makes us love people and animals, and helps us to see all the things that are beautiful in the world, whether it's all the stars in the sky or tiny flowers in the grass.

A Every time we want to do something good, that's God; every time we feel love, that's God. Everybody feels love for something sometime, and God is that feeling. You can't see God, but because lots of people feel love, love is everywhere and so is God. Some people believe that God started the world, and there are different stories of how God made all the plants, animals, and people.

A God isn't a man or a woman and God isn't black or white, because God isn't a person. God doesn't have a house like ours, because God is everywhere and in everything. God is like a very good and powerful spirit. People started to think about God thousands of years ago. Some people believe there are lots of gods, but the Jews were the first people to believe in just one God for everybody. Jesus was a Jew whom Christians believe is God in the form of a man. People say God is in heaven, but that isn't a place in the sky. Heaven is a way to describe the special feeling of goodness some people believe they will find with God after they have died.

A Thousands of years ago, people who lived in different places each developed a different idea of God or lots of gods, so there are many gods and different ways of worshiping. Most Christians believe that Jesus really was God in the form of a man and that there is no difference between God the Father and God the Son – but that by becoming man and suffering in the same way as lots of people do in the world, God would show how much he loved everybody. Some people also believe that there's a force for evil in the world, which has been given various names such as the Devil, who is said to live in a place called hell. But since the Devil is not a person, no one can say for sure what hell really is. People who believe in a god are "believers"; those who don't are "nonbelievers," or "atheists," and those who aren't sure are called "agnostics."

Nigerian ancestor god

Jesus Christ

Buddha

Osiris, Egyptian god

Ganesha, Hindu god of wisdom

Q What is religion?

- *How are there so many religions?* ● *Which religion is right?*
- *Why do people from different religions fight one another?*
- *Do all religions believe in God?*

Answering questions about other religions positively will help your children to be tolerant as well as broadening their view beyond the immediate environment of home and school. Help your children by pointing out the similarities within the different traditions, through examples like the various creation myths and stories.

WHAT'S BEHIND THIS QUESTION

These questions indicate that your child has discovered there are different religions and traditions from those followed by your family. Most younger children will ask because they are genuinely curious – just as they want to know why there are basic differences between boys and girls, they also want to know why their friends may lead different lives and believe different things. However, if the questions imply that they have picked up concepts of "better/worse" and "superior/inferior" – and older children may have received this from other children or their families – then you should be careful to prevent your child having such an outlook on life and other people; religious intolerance is often associated with racism and bullying.

GUIDELINES FOR YOUR ANSWERS

- Questions about religious beliefs give you an opportunity to teach your child tolerance and love of humanity, which is common to most religious faiths.
- Try to teach comparative religion. Even if you yourself have a strong religious faith and you do not agree with the beliefs of a different religion, you can still acknowledge the right of others to worship as they

wish, and point out that different religions should not be in competition with one another.

- It's natural to bring your children up in your own faith, but make it clear that when they are older and able to think about religion for themselves, they will be welcome to choose whichever faith they wish.
- Squash anything that resembles racist thinking or bully tactics. Teach equality and fairness.

WHAT ELSE TO KNOW

- Children will note the difference in color of someone's skin or in the way they worship, but they don't think of it as a mark of superiority or inferiority. It's we adults who teach that.
- Left to themselves, children of all nationalities and beliefs play together and get along very well. It is adults who introduce bias and prejudice.
- Develop your child's innate sense of fairness and build on her unprejudiced view of the world and people. Ask her, "What do you think?"

People pray in many ways
Everyone should be free to worship in their own way.

Other things you may be asked...

- *Are all religions just as good?*
- *Are you friends with people from other religions?*
- *Does our God take care of them?*
- *Why do they go to church/temple on a different day?*
- *Why do some religious people wear special clothes?*

See also *Why isn't my skin brown? p. 68* ● *What happens when you die? p. 40* ● *What is God? p. 44*

A Because people come from different places all over the world they live in different ways and do different things. They also have different Gods that they believe in: for instance, Christians have Christ and Hindus have Vishnu.

A When people decide to follow special rules about what kind of God they believe in, it's called religion. People of the same religion pray to their God in special places. Sometimes they wear particular clothes or have their hair in a special way. People believe in different kinds of God, or the same God in a different way, but we should all get along and try to learn more about each other.

A People from all over the world think about God and have written about their ideas of God in their own books. People who are part of the same religion share their beliefs in God and a way of worshiping. Most religions set aside a certain day of the week for worship, as well as special occasions such as Christmas, Ramadam, or Diwali. We have friends who belong to different religions – David and Margot are Jewish, Jill and Bob are Buddhists, and Yindi and Nabeel are Muslims. People believe that following their religion will help them to lead better and more caring lives.

A Sometimes the believers of a particular religion thought everyone else should believe it so they tried to convert them. They even thought people were wicked if they didn't follow the same religion, so they punished them or went to war against them. Some people still see others who believe in different religions as enemies, even if they are not interested in trying to convert them. But everyone should be free to follow a religion and worship God without being troubled, because it's a private matter for you alone to decide. You can still be a good person without believing in God at all, or belonging to any particular religion. You can decide later when you've have had time to think about it. We'll still love you, whatever you decide.

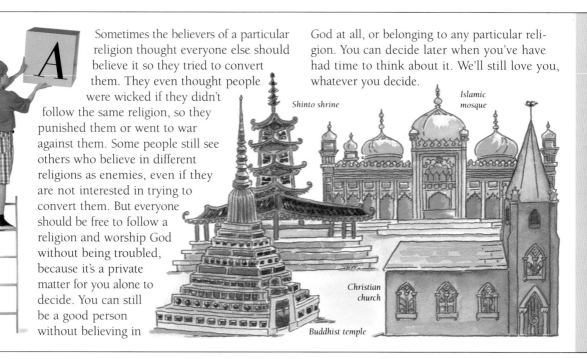

Shinto shrine

Islamic mosque

Christian church

Buddhist temple

Q Will I be safe in the dark?

- *Can I sleep with the light on?* ● *What are ghosts?*
- *Will a monster hide in my room in the dark?*
- *How do I know scary things won't come?*

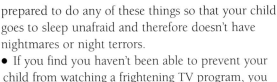

Irrational fears are not exclusive to childhood, of course, but children are particularly prone to them as they try to make sense of new experiences. Small children with vivid imaginations may transform apparently banal or even happy images into objects of fear, and their fears need sensitive responses to avoid long-term problems.

WHAT'S BEHIND THIS QUESTION

It's very easy to imagine all kinds of horrors in the dark as we all know, and adulthood doesn't necessarily bring immunity to irrational fears. So it's not surprising that some children are frightened of the dark, of monsters, witches, dragons, and creepy crawlies. Children have active imaginations, and as far as they are concerned all these things are real because fantasy is difficult to separate from reality. Seeing shadows on the wall and hearing creaks on the stairs only seem to convince your child that his worst fears are confirmed. Be alert to frightening TV programs and films, and the more gruesome fairy stories, which may quite unexpectedly trigger some irrational fear. Even clowns or masked characters can disturb susceptible children.

GUIDELINES FOR YOUR ANSWERS

- It's intelligent to be afraid of the dark, it's not silly or weak; never make fun of your child for being afraid.
- Help your child to overcome his fears by finding out what you can do to be reassuring. It may be a nightlight or a light left on in the hall, or occasionally you could stay with your child until he's asleep. Be

prepared to do any of these things so that your child goes to sleep unafraid and therefore doesn't have nightmares or night terrors.

- If you find you haven't been able to prevent your child from watching a frightening TV program, you can help to avoid nightmares if you bring your child back into the real world by doing something mundane like teeth cleaning, hair brushing, or planning tomorrow's lunch. Or you can talk positively about something really good that happened, or anticipate an exciting and happy event, like a birthday party or vacation. Once they were over the age of nine, and after the usual good nights, all my children went to sleep listening to their own musical selection, which prevented frightening thoughts.
- Reassure your child with your voice as he goes to sleep by keeping up a running commentary from another room.

WHAT ELSE TO KNOW

- Many frightening memories arise from images or fantasies in the dark. Your child can't verbalize them and you'll never know what they are. Simply respect your child's fears and be sympathetic, consoling, and reassuring at all times.
- Help your child get over a shock by letting him go to sleep while lying down next to you, or starting the night in your bed. He can go back to his own room when he's more confident. Try switching the furniture around in his bedroom so it looks and feels different.

Other things you may be asked...

- *Can you talk to people who are dead?*
- *Are any spirits kind?*
- *How will I know there's no one outside my room?*
- *Can monsters hurt me?*
- *Is there someone in the closet?*

See also *What happens when you die? p. 40* ● *What does violence mean? p. 84*

A You can have a nightlight or I'll leave the light on outside. Don't worry, no one will hurt you – Mommy and Daddy are here. I'll go out and keep talking to you for a little while so you know I'm here. Just shout "Good night, Mommy and Daddy," and we'll shout "good night" back.

A Ghosts and witches and monsters and giants and dragons aren't real – they're just make-believe, in stories. Because they aren't real, they can't come in the dark. You remember how Bandit always barks if someone comes or he hears something? Well, why don't we get him to lie outside your door and he'll keep you safe. If you don't believe in ghosts and monsters, they can't hurt you, can they?

A There's no one in your closet; let's go look. There's nothing there! Now we'll close the door together so we both know that nothing could possibly get in. And we'll look under the bed and behind the curtains just to make you feel better. Dad and I won't be far away – we'll be in the living room, don't worry. But just this once you can keep your reading light on for a while. Let's find a book with a happy story. Put your books away at 8:30 and turn the light down low. You can listen to quiet music as you go to sleep. I'll check to see that you're all right before I go to bed.

A That was a bad dream – but it wasn't real – it was only a dream. It was probably just because you watched that television show about the space-ship, wasn't it? You know that was just a story – with actors and special effects – that looked real but was really pretend. We could get a book out of the library to understand how it's done.

Why don't I keep you company before you go back to sleep and we'll talk about some good times when you really enjoyed yourself, like when we went to the fair: What was your favorite ride? Do you remember the sun was shining and the sky was blue and the flags were waving? We could see from the top of the ferris wheel all the way over to the other side of he park, and you had the money for ice cream in your pocket.

QUESTIONS ABOUT

Can I miss school for once?

Where's Mom gone?

Is it my fault?

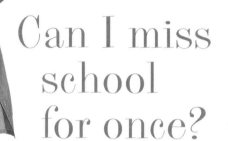

Why do I always get the blame?

Am I adopted?

Why can't Daddy live with us?

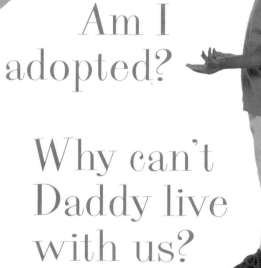

● SEPARATION ● DIVORCE ● STEP-PARENTING ● ADOPTION ●

RELATIONSHIPS

A child's world revolves around close personal relationships, first at home with parents and siblings and then at school with friends and teachers. Changes, problems, or arguments with any of these can have a profound effect on children, in ways that may be difficult

How can I make friends?

for them to articulate. Although in all probability your child's questions are very straightforward, be alert to the possible scenarios behind them. At first glance, these may not appear to relate directly to the problem or uncertainty that is really bothering them, and you may need to probe gently to get to the source. But if you suspect anything out of the ordinary, try to discover the real reason for your child's concern without provoking antagonism or feelings of guilt. These can be damaging to a child, especially one who is coming to terms with emotional turmoil, so try to clarify your child's anxieties and give simple, straightforward answers. The questions here are united by a threat to your child's security, even though the circumstances may differ. When your six-year-old daughter has an argument with

What's divorce?

her best friend, she may be as devastated as another child who has to cope with his parents' divorce. It is all a question of degree – but what is really important is that your love and reassurance provide the cornerstone to your answers.

Q Where did Mommy/Daddy go?

- *Doesn't Mommy/Daddy love you anymore?*
- *Why do you and Mommy/Daddy fight?*
- *Why does Mommy/Daddy sleep in the spare room now?*

Trying to protect children caught in the middle of the breakdown of their parents' relationship can be heartbreaking for both mother and father. However, being as honest as you can when you answer their questions is one way to help them feel secure in your love for them, in spite of what is happening between you as a couple. Try not to bad-mouth a partner, no matter what your personal feelings may be – that person is still your child's other parent.

WHAT'S BEHIND THIS QUESTION

Problems arise in all relationships; in learning that Mom and Dad may not always be the best of friends, your child is learning a lesson about life. He is fine as long as he is confident of your mutual love, but when he first realizes your relationship is troubled he may feel that his whole world is breaking down, or that that he can't trust anyone if he cannot rely on his parents. Children in this situation frequently become insecure, may regress, become mischievous, and attention-seeking for reassurance, and they nearly always blame themselves for what's happened.

GUIDELINES FOR YOUR ANSWERS

- If you go through a troubled time with your partner, reassure your child that you both still love him, no matter what happens. If you manage to patch things up, include your child in the reconciliation so that everyone in the family can feel united.

- Whether or not there is a permanent breakup, it's essential that children feel secure about their future. Reassure them that they will be safe even if their mother or father has left.
- Children often worry about things that never occur to us, like who will take them to school. Always ask what's worrying them, always tell the truth in a way they can understand, and, once they're old enough, warn them about what's going to happen – don't spring things on them at the last minute.
- The answers here are from the point of view of a father who is separating from his partner; you can adjust your answers to suit your situation if necessary.

WHAT ELSE TO KNOW

- Your child will soak up emotional signals; if you're sad, the chances are he will be, too.
- Children want to be told about breakups; if they're kept in the dark, they stop trusting and respecting you.
- Don't think your child won't know what's going on, or try to shield him from it. Children feel insecure if they only know part of the story.
- For the partner that moves out: Tell your child you're not taking your love with you and you'll write, call, and visit often. If possible, give him a specific date to plan for and never let him down.
- By continuing to visit regularly and helping to maintain a child's routine, grandparents, other family members, and close friends can be wonderful in reassuring a child that his family still exists and loves him.

Other things you may be asked...

- *Why are you shouting at each other?*
- *Does that mean Mommy/Daddy doesn't love me anymore?*
- *Why do people stop loving each other?*
- *Is it my fault?*
- *Will Mommy/Daddy come back?*

See also *What's a divorce? p. 54* • *Do I have to call him Daddy? p. 56*

FOR AGES 2–4

AMommy and Daddy are angry with each other so Mommy may decide to go away and live somewhere else for a while. Mommy's really sad she can't be with you, but we both still love you very much and always will. Mommy will come and see you very soon – at least once a week.

FOR AGES 4–6

AMommy and Daddy are very angry with each other at the moment and it's difficult to sleep next to someone if you're angry with them. Mommies and Daddies don't always stay together forever. Sometimes they find they don't love each other anymore. It's going to be difficult for Mommy to leave you because she still loves you, but she'll come back to see you every week. Remember, it's not your fault.

FOR AGES 6–8

AMommy and Daddy are not living together right now. We disagree about things and we don't like being angry with each other all the time, especially because we know it upsets you. We're going to try and work things out so we can all live together again, but we may not be able to. Even though we're trying very hard, we could find that it's impossible to live together. Mommy hasn't stopped loving you, and it isn't your fault – you're not to blame. She didn't leave because you were bad. I'm here to take care of you, and Mommy will visit you every week. She loves you very much.

FOR AGES 8–11

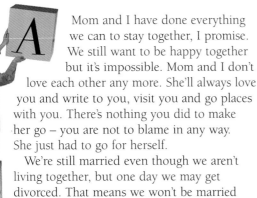

AMom and I have done everything we can to stay together, I promise. We still want to be happy together but it's impossible. Mom and I don't love each other any more. She'll always love you and write to you, visit you and go places with you. There's nothing you did to make her go – you are not to blame in any way. She just had to go for herself.

We're still married even though we aren't living together, but one day we may get divorced. That means we won't be married to each other any more, but we'll never stop being your Mom and Dad, and we'll never stop loving you. We might still do things together, like going to movies and seeing you in school plays, and going out for meals and baseball games.

Q What's a divorce?

- *Why are you and Daddy getting divorced?*
- *Why can't we still live together?* • *Do you have to get divorced?*
- *Was Daddy mean to you?* • *Will I still be able to see Daddy?*

Divorce is never easy for a couple, but when there are children involved it is much harder for all concerned. Whatever the circumstances of a divorce, children need reassurance that their needs will be met, that they are not to blame for the breakdown of their parents' marriage and that both their parents will continue to love them as before.

WHAT'S BEHIND THIS QUESTION

Doubt is one of the worst feelings for a child, leading to fear and confusion, so never leave your child in any doubt that you both love her and, whatever happens, she will continue to be cared for at home by one of you. It's very revealing talking to children whose parents have been through a divorce; children always want to know that they are not to blame, that they're still loved by both parents, and, if possible, that their parents remain friends (and act like friends). When asked about our divorce, one of my sons said, "It was okay, Mom, I could handle it because you and Dad were obviously still friends." For this section, the questions are answered from the point of view of a mother who has care of the children, with the father absent. As before, adjust the answers to your own circumstances.

GUIDELINES FOR YOUR ANSWERS

- Because children under five perceive the world in relation to themselves, it's best to explain at least partially what's going on, even at this tender age. If you don't, children will invent their own explanations, mistakenly blaming themselves for problems in the family.

- If you don't give a plausible explanation of why you and your partner are divorcing, your child may come up with her own wild explanations, such as "Mommy left because I don't keep my room clean," or "Daddy was mad because I wet the bed/I am clumsy/I can't do math/I lost my allowance."
- Feelings of guilt are damaging for a child already coming to terms with the insecurity that a breakup can trigger. Ask questions to clarify your child's anxieties and give simple, straightforward answers.
- Whatever the circumstances of your divorce, and no matter how bitter you may feel, try not to transmit this to your child. Your child is half of each partner and will feel worthless if you vent your dislike and anger for her parent.

WHAT ELSE TO KNOW

- If you become a single parent, try not to be upset when your child misses her absent parent. Avoid pretending that he or she doesn't exist.
- Tell your child's teachers what's happened and ask them to keep a close eye on her to avert difficulties at school. Give your child space to voice worries; listen to her and take them seriously.
- Older children may worry about having enough money. Divorce does strain many families' finances, but try not to burden your child with it. It could provide another reason for her to feel guilty.

Other things you may be asked...

- *Do you and Daddy still love me?*
- *Will Daddy still love me when you're divorced?*
- *Will I still be able to see Grandma and Grandpa?*
- *Will I still go to the same school?*

See also Do I have to call him Daddy? p. 56 • Where did Mommy/Daddy go? p. 52

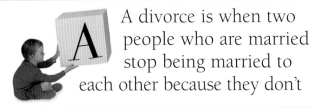

A divorce is when two people who are married stop being married to each other because they don't love each other anymore. We're getting divorced, but we still love you very much and we'll take care of you just the same.

Mommy and Daddy are getting divorced because they really can't work things out to stay together. We'll still be friends because that's best for all of us. Mommy and Daddy will always love you and take care of you. I know you love us both and you'll be able to have time with both of us, I promise. Daddy will have a different home but even if you don't see him every day he'll still love you.

Divorce is sad. Nobody wants to split up a family; that's why I'm sad now and then. We would still like the family to stay together but Daddy feels he needs to make a fresh start. He doesn't blame you for anything. Mommy and Daddy don't love each other anymore – that's why we're unkind to each other sometimes. Grown-ups sometimes stop loving each other; they change from when they got married, especially if they were quite young then. But we'll never stop loving you – we both love you very much and we'll try not to be unkind to you. You will still spend time with Daddy very often – you can help best if you tell him you love him and will see him soon.

Nobody wants a divorce – Mom and Dad tried really hard to avoid it but we've decided we have to make a change. Dad will eventually move out on his own and you'll stay here with me. He'll miss you a lot, but he'll still love you like he always has and he'll write you letters and postcards and call and see you every other weekend and on some holidays. We think it's best for you to live with me so you can stay at the same school and be close to all your friends. Don't worry, I'll still take you to school and we will have enough money. When you're old enough you can decide for yourself whether you live with Mom or Dad. Why not speak to Steve at school – his parents are divorced – and then ask me some more questions.

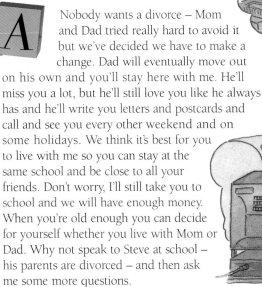

Q Do I have to call him Daddy?

- *Do you love me as much as Sarah and Tom?*

- *Why can't I live with my real Mommy/Daddy?*

- *Why can't Daddy still live with us?*

If you are a single parent who has started a relationship, it can be painful if your child finds it difficult to accept your new partner. However, it's a natural reaction, so everyone involved needs to be patient, understanding and willing to compromise for the greater good – winning your child's trust.

WHAT'S BEHIND THIS QUESTION

Nothing can dislodge the central role that parents play in a child's life, so when a child is confronted by a prospective stepparent, confusion and unhappiness can be the result. A child may become very insecure, mistrustful of all adults and need a lot of reassurance. A child's anxiety at losing the estranged parent altogether can be intense, particularly if he feels that the new stepparent is going to usurp the natural parent's position – the classic fairy tale scenario. All aspects of the life of a child in this situation may be affected: he may stop eating, start having nightmares, become rebellious and start failing at school. If there are stepbrothers and sisters, or a new baby is on the way, your child may worry that you will withdraw your love and transfer it to the new members of the family.

GUIDELINES FOR YOUR ANSWERS

- When you and a new partner enter into a long-term relationship, whether or not you remarry, your main goal should be to reassure your child with words and actions which show very clearly that you still love him and always will, no matter what. You may have to repeat this over and over. Tell him at least once a day how special he is, especially last thing at night.
- When you're introducing a stepparent to your child, do not criticize the biological parent. Present your new partner as a bonus. It's not surprising that children have difficulty with the concept of two sets of parents. When he acquired me as a stepmother, my stepson's problems were solved when he found other friends at school who had two "Dads."
- Never talk about "Your new Mommy/Daddy" as if your child's real parent no longer exists. A younger child especially may see this as a rejection of his natural parent and may fear that he will not be able to see the absent parent.
- I have answered the questions from the point of view of a mother introducing a new partner who has children of his own. Adapt this to your own situation.

WHAT ELSE TO KNOW

- Never force the pace of acceptance; go at the child's speed. A stepparent's initial aim should be to make friends. If closeness follows, all well and good.
- Try to minimize tension between the stepparent and absent parent. A stepparent should expect few parental rights – you can't replace the biological parent, nor should you want to. I used to encourage my stepsons to see their mother when they wanted and not conform to formal visitations. As a stepparent you don't want to be remembered for jealousy or resentment.

Other things you may be asked...

- *Can I still see my Mommy/Daddy?*

- *Does he/she have to live with us?*

- *What's a half-sister/-brother?*

- *What's a stepsister/-brother?*

See also *Where did Mommy/Daddy go? p. 52* • *What's a divorce? p. 54*

A Alex is Mommy's new husband. He's coming to live here with us and will help me take care of you. He's looking forward to getting to know you even better. Daddy knows about him and you'll see Daddy just as much as before.

A stepparent is a person who marries someone who already has children. The stepparent isn't a real Mommy/Daddy, but helps to take care of you. Both kinds of parents love you. You don't have to call your stepfather "Daddy" – you can use his first name. I love your stepfather, but your Daddy is still very special to you, and you can see him and talk with him as often as you like.

A It's difficult to understand having two sets of Mommies and Daddies, but it happens quite often. Why not ask some of your friends if they have a stepmom or stepdad? It's nice to think that there's another grown-up at home who loves you just as much as his own children, Sarah and Tom. They're your stepbrother and stepsister – their Mommy and Daddy are different from yours, but we love you all just the same. If Alex and I decide to have a baby, he or she will be your half-brother or -sister because the baby will grow in Mommy's tummy, like you did, but have a different father. And the baby will be Tom and Sarah's half-brother too, so you can share him.

A Your real Dad is one of the people who made you and I want you to love him and see and stay with him as often as possible, because he loves you as much as I do. Alex is your stepdad. He wants to be your friend, but he knows he can't take the place of your real Dad. Alex and I both want to make this change as easy as possible for you.

No matter what happens, your real Mom and Dad can't be changed, and we'll always love you. We'll try to do whatever we can to help you. You can always be honest with me and tell me all about your fears or bad feelings – I promise not to be angry, because it's important to say how you really feel. It's hard to accept a new situation, but we're all going to work together at being happy.

Q Why am I adopted?

- *Am I adopted?* • *Are you my real Mommy and Daddy?*
- *Who are my parents?* • *Can I see my birth Mom and Dad?*
- *How can I have two Mommies and two Daddies?*

If you have adopted a child, it is important to reassure her that your love is even stronger than the birth parents' love. Answering your child's questions honestly and making sure she knows the truth as soon as possible will help avoid the trauma of sudden discovery. You should talk about your child being adopted from the very beginning so that it's accepted as normal.

——— WHAT'S BEHIND THIS QUESTION ———

The advice to the majority of parents who adopt a baby is to let your child know as early as possible that she is adopted, in a way that fits her age and understanding. Questions will naturally arise from this early knowledge as your child begins to connect her understanding of how babies are made to her own situation. At this point she will look for extra reassurance that you really love her, and that you aren't going to give her away, like her birth parents had to in the first place. If you adopt an older child who can remember her life before she came into your family, you may find the questions arise because the child wants to know why you chose to adopt her, rather than any other child. Children in this situation may have an underlying insecurity that may take years to counteract. They could continue to worry that if their adoptive parents get angry, they might be sent away again.

——— GUIDELINES FOR YOUR ANSWERS ———

- Like questions about sex and death, questions from your adopted child should not be shirked, because there is a danger that she may learn about the adoption from someone else – possibly even in a moment of anger. This could destroy your child's confidence in you, which, as adoptive parents, you will have painstakingly built up over the years.
- Always answer a question about adoption frankly and honestly: every person has the right to know who their parents are, irrespective of age. Even if your child doesn't ask, offer the information when she is young, at three or four, in a matter-of-fact way, so that she accepts it calmly.
- When children learn that their birth mother gave them up for adoption, they may feel worthless. You will need to demonstrate your affection in much more overt ways while they adjust to the idea.
- Always praise your child's birth mother, stressing the courage she needed to give her child a better life, and how incredibly lucky and privileged you feel to take over as your child's parents.

——— WHAT ELSE TO KNOW ———

- There are several organizations that help birth parents and adult children to find each other. If your child asks questions about her birth parents, you may wish to offer to help find them when the time comes. Be sure to keep your promise.
- Tell your child from your heart why you adopted her and she will feel secure in your love and grow up with plenty of confidence and strong self-esteem.

Other things you may be asked...

- *Will you always love me?*
- *Why did you adopt me?*
- *Why did she give me away?*
- *Do my first Mommy and Daddy love me?*
- *Will you always be my Daddy?*
- *Are you angry with me because I'm adopted?*

See also *Where did I come from? p. 12* • *Why do I always get the blame? p. 60*

FOR AGES 2–4

Children under age four will rarely ask this question unless they have been recently adopted and the word has been used about them. If a mature 3½-year-old raises the subject, base your answers on the 4–6 age group, below.

FOR AGES 4–6

A You have two Mommies and Daddies because the Daddy and Mommy who made you weren't able to take care of you, which was very sad for them. So another Mommy and Daddy were found to look after you – that's us – and we think we are very lucky. Don't worry, you'll always stay with us. We love you and take care of you because we are your Mommy and Daddy, and we always will be.

FOR AGES 6–8

A If you want, I'll help you find out who your real Mommy and Daddy are when you're grown up. I believe you should try to find them. I can't say why your real Mommy gave you up, but it wasn't because she didn't love you. It was a very hard thing for her to do. I expect she'll be pleased to see you if you ever meet when you're a grown-up. We adopted you because we can't make any children of our own but we know that there are lots of babies and children whose parents unfortunately aren't able to look after them. We wanted very much to give a home to one of those babies. We thought you were lovely when we first met you – and we always will.

FOR AGES 8–11

A If you want, you can find out who your real birth parents are when you're old enough – I'll help you find them. I'm sure your Mom loved you. She offered you for adoption because she had no choice and couldn't take care of you. She loved you so much she wanted you to have a better life with people who could take care of you and love you just as much. I feel sure she'll be pleased to see you when you're grown up.

I would never be angry with you just because you're adopted – but I would get mad if you didn't do your schoolwork or if you didn't tell the truth. Ask Jane – her Mom and Dad get angry with her sometimes, too! We love you and want the best for you like all parents do for their children.

Q Why do I always get the blame?

- *Do you love him more than me?* • *Why's she your favorite?*
- *Why's he never wrong?* • *Why am I always the naughty one?*
- *Do you wish I was more like her?*

Trying to be fair when you have more than one child is one of the most difficult tasks for parents. Each child in the family wants to feel special, and will be quick to show resentment if he feels that another child is being favored by either parent.

WHAT'S BEHIND THIS QUESTION

Sibling rivalry is a reality and, as some children are prone to insecurity about their parents' long-term love, they may pick up all sorts of nuances that adults discount. Once they feel any hint of preference for a sibling, they will see confirmation of your favoritism in a thousand other small incidents. I would never allow an older child to be rough with a younger one, so the youngsters were always seen as protected and preferred. But that's a lesson for life – a strong aggressor can never be allowed to intimidate a weaker victim.

On the other hand, a younger child might feel resentful that she has to go to bed earlier than an older sibling, or isn't allowed to watch a particular TV program. Very often such questions are a warning that your child is feeling left out, even unloved. You should act quickly to reassure her in word and deed, by spending dedicated time with the aggrieved child each day and repeating that you love him all the time.

GUIDELINES FOR YOUR ANSWERS

- Although you can answer your child's questions with explanations, actions always mean more – big hugs, time spent alone with him, arranging private outings, admiring a new skill, a special bedtime story.

- The main message to give is that you're fair and even; though your child may perceive injustices or imbalances, it will all balance out in the end. I tried to teach my four children to think in a longer timescale than one hour or one day and they learned to trust me; it might take a year but they'd all get their turn at being the special one. Children love you unconditionally: they deserve some of that back.
- Stress each child's unique individuality – be positive about their different strengths.

WHAT ELSE TO KNOW

Unfortunately life's not always fair. Home is the best place to learn this rather unpalatable truth. My sons were not all equally good at making friends. The outgoing, loving ones seemed to have a better time socially compared with the introspective loners. That's a hard fact of life, so we had to think up ways of compensating for the discrepancies that suited each child, and we didn't always get it right. Once a child was old enough we explained our fallibility. "Life's tough" were words used quite often in our house.

Other things you may be asked...

- *Why does he always get the best toys?*
- *Why does she always get more candy?*
- *Why don't you ever tell her off?*
- *Why do you let him stay home from school and not me?*
- *Why is her piece always bigger than mine?*

See also *Do I have to call him Daddy? p. 56* • *Why am I adopted? p. 58* • *What's a bully? p. 82*

A We're not really angry with you all the time. It might seem that way because you remember when we *are* angry and forget all the times that we're happy and proud. We're very lucky to have you as our little boy. After playgroup I'll take you to the park without the baby, just you and me.

A You don't always get the blame, but as you get older you learn what is not right, and you can learn to stop yourself. Sara is younger than you so she doesn't know what's right or wrong just yet. You're much bigger than her; we probably expect you to be more grown-up and that's not fair, because you remember to be good so much of the time. We love you very much, always.

A I know it's hard for you to go to bed earlier than Jennie, but she is older than you and doesn't need as much sleep. It isn't because we like her more than you, it's because you get very tired when you stay up late and then you don't enjoy yourself at school the next day. We want you to be happy and do well. Jennie's only allowed to stay up and watch the nature program, and then she's going to bed as well because she needs her rest too. During vacation you can stay up late sometimes, too, because then you'll be able to sleep later in the morning.

A I know he's the baby and he tends to get away with things, but you spoil him, too, don't you? You peel his orange and give him the best parts and when he's tired you put him on your shoulders. The baby in the family often gets spoiled by the whole family. But if it really feels unfair, speak up and I'll do something about it. He probably is allowed to do some things at a younger age than you were but you were our first baby and we had to learn about taking care of children through you. Now we've learned more, so we may be more relaxed with our younger kids. But you are the oldest and so you're very special to us. You're such a wonderful big sister, I think you've earned some special privileges. You can stop sharing a room with Anna and we'll redecorate your own room just the way you want. You can take your friends there. I have never wished you were anyone else – I love you for what you are.

Q Why can't I make friends?

- *Why don't I have a best friend?* ● *Why doesn't anybody like me?*
- *Why does Susan tease me?* ● *Why won't anyone play with me?*
- *Why do they laugh at me at school?*

From school age, your child's friendships are very important to his emotional and social development. Some children naturally make lots of friends, and others prefer to stick steadfastly to one particular person. Sometimes things go temporarily wrong, but if your child really seems to have difficulty in making or keeping friends, you may have to take a few sensitive but positive steps to help.

WHAT'S BEHIND THIS QUESTION

Your child may be a natural loner and be very happy flying solo. Such children are often self-sufficient and independent; they have played alone happily since infancy, are easily engaged by toys, games, and books; and often learn to read very early. They don't need or miss friends, but once they enter the social structure of school, such children can be seen as "different" by classmates who tend to isolate them. Your child will be sensitive to that. Then there are the frequent and normal squabbles about best friends: "No, Patty isn't YOUR best friend, she's MINE!" Even four-year-olds can be hurt by being excluded. Most children enjoy having friends from as early as age two, but later on, at school, these questions may sometimes be associated with bullying. It is worth probing gently, using my guidelines on bullying on page 82.

GUIDELINES FOR YOUR ANSWERS

- Encourage your child's social skills from an early age by teaching him to share and to be gentle and friendly. Remember that an unloved child can't do these things.
- From the age of five, many children select a favorite playmate, so try to invite different children over to play or on outings, so that he has lots of kids to choose from.
- You can't force another child to be friendly with yours, but when a child is over to play, involve yourself in their activities (as appropriate), so that you can check that your child's response is appropriate.
- If your child is a loner but wants friends, try giving him more responsibility to boost his confidence. Discuss with your child's teacher the possibility of giving him and a suitable partner a job, like passing out paper, as this confers status among his peers.

WHAT ELSE TO KNOW

- By the time your child is four, he can probably play with other children in an imaginative, sustained way. At this age, gender is not usually a criterion for friendship – and neither is race or dress, so keep your child's circle of friends mixed.
- Having an imaginary friend who is occasionally used as a scapegoat is a normal part of a younger child's development, so be patient and tolerant. By the age of seven or eight, children usually grow out of this phase and clearly know the difference between fantasy and reality. If it persists, it could be a sign of loneliness.
- From the age of six, school and peer groups may have more influence on your child than home and parents, so always consult teachers about how best to tackle friendship issues. Together you can help your child find the best approach to making friends.

Other things you may be asked...

- *How can I have a best friend?*
- *How can I make friends?*
- *Why doesn't John want to play?*
- *Why doesn't anyone pick me for their team?*
- *Why can't you see my (imaginary) friend?*

See also *Why do I have to go to school? p. 64* ● *What's a bully? p. 82*

A It's nice to share things with friends. We'll play with Barbara in the playroom, then you and Barbara can have a tea party. Tomorrow we could have John, Chris, and Kate over, and you can all share your toys.

A There's nothing wrong with being quiet. I'll bet there's someone else who likes drawing and reading books in the book corner, isn't there? Maybe Jack would go with you to the school library at lunchtime. We could ask your teacher. Friends are nice; they're company, you have fun together, and enjoy the same things. You don't have to have lots of friends – we'll invite your closest friends over after school for your birthday party.

A Maria has lots of different friends; she might feel a little uncomfortable if you want her to play only with you at school. Invite her over on Saturday instead so you can have lots of time together.
    I've never met your imaginary friend, have I? That's because she's in your mind and I can't see in there. It's nice for you to have someone private to talk to and play with, because you don't feel lonely. It's also a good idea to have your own real friends, too. We can invite Rosie for lunch, even though your imaginary friend doesn't like her.

A Sometimes it's difficult to know why you don't have more friends. Mostly it's about being friendly to others. People want other people to take an interest in them, so if you let them know that you're interested in what they think, they'll often be glad to make friends with you. If you hang back and don't speak up, they might think that you're happier on your own even though they really would like to be your friends. You need to send out the opposite kind of message and ask "Can I join in?"
    But you don't *need* to have a lot of friends. If you'd like to make more friends, we could try a few ideas: We could ask some of your classmates over to see a movie or go out for pizza, or I could tape the game for you to watch with a friend. You can always have a friend sleep over, too, if you like. Just think about it.

Q Why do I have to go to school?

- *Why do I have to go to play group/nursery school?*
- *Do I have to go to the same school as Tommy Jones?*
- *Do I have to be in Miss Smith's class?*

It's natural for younger children to be a little reluctant about leaving home to go to day care, nursery school, or school, especially to start with. But parents need to be alert to problems that occur after the initial settling-in period. With older children already in school for some years, there may be deeper problems that need to be handled sensitively.

——— WHAT'S BEHIND THIS QUESTION ———

It could be simply a grumble, a challenge, in which case you have to be firm and talk about the good things about school, accentuating the positive aspects that your child has enjoyed in the past. A child starting nursery or full-time school for the first time is bound to need a period of adjustment, but some questions require further probing. For instance "Can I have some more money for school?" raises the possibility of playground extortion, or even truancy. The former may be a sign that your child is being bullied and victimized; the latter, a sign of boredom; either way, the problem needs your attention. True school phobia – an irrational fear of school – is very rare, but keep it at the back of your mind if your child gets sick from fear of school. You may need professional help.

——— GUIDELINES FOR YOUR ANSWERS ———

- Learning to take the rough with the smooth, to take criticism, is a great basic lesson in life, and school is the place where your child can learn these invaluable lessons with your help, in partnership with the staff at your children's school.

- Always be ready to listen and sympathize; let your child know that you are prepared to solve problems.
- Your child may ask you to bend school rules, or make excuses for his proposed absences: mine did. My answer was always the same – we may not always agree with all school rules, but they serve a purpose and we keep them as best we can during school time.
- If the questions reveal bullying or truancy, you should always report it to your child's teacher and follow up to make sure it is being dealt with properly. (See my guidelines on page 82.)

——— WHAT ELSE TO KNOW ———

- Children under eight have difficulty pinning down what's wrong. Once my seven-year-old came home from school looking glum; when I asked why, he said, "The world doesn't feel right." It turned out he was worried because he couldn't learn his multiplication tables.
- If the problem stems from dislike or fear of a staff member, talk to your child's teacher first, even if he or she is the one your child has named. A child may be transferring his nervousness about school onto that person. If there isn't any improvement after this discussion, take your concerns to the principal.
- The arrival of a new baby may make a young child reluctant to go to school – he may feel rejected or jealous when he sees that the baby can stay at home with you. Try to organize a division of labor so that one parent stays with the baby and the other takes the child to school so he can have a special time with you.

Other things you may be asked...

- *Why can't you always take me to school?*
- *Can I go and play with Jenny instead of going to school?*
- *Can I have more money for school?*
- *Can I miss school for once?*
- *Why can't I stay here with you and the baby?*

See also *Why can't I make friends? p. 62* • *What's a bully? p. 82*

A At nursery school you'll see all your friends and play with the toys we don't have at home. I'll stay with you a little while today and then you can bring a friend home to play. You can help me choose what to have for snack.

A Daddy's going to stay behind with baby Jane, but you're such a big smart boy, I'm going to take you to school so you can show me all the things you do. It'll be a long time before Jane will be big enough to do them. I know school can be tiring, but there's lots of new things to do. Teachers can seem a little strict because they have so many children to look after but they're really very nice.

A Going to school to learn is mostly about being happy and doing things you like. If you learn well you'll be able to choose whatever you want to do when you're older, so it's worth working hard now. You told me you'd like to be a rocket scientist – no one can become one of those if they don't learn how to write and read, and to understand numbers. I'm sure your teacher likes you very much, and wants you to be happy in school. What's happened to make you think she might not? Are you sure she wasn't just upset about something else? If there's something you don't understand, we can talk it out at home and I'll talk to your teacher about it later.

A It would be better if you didn't take a day off because you'll miss work and have to make it up later. Is something wrong at school? If you missed school today you'd miss art as well, which would be too bad, because you enjoy it. Not everyone is friendly at school and some teachers don't always make lessons interesting, but we have to take the good with the bad. Dad and Mom often work with people we might not choose to be friends with, but we still have to be polite. Why do you want more money? Does Rob take it? Next time he does, tell me or your teacher right away and we'll go and see the principal.

QUESTIONS ABOUT

Why isn't my skin brown?

Will she get better?

What does racism mean?

Why is that girl's hair so curly?

Was he born like that?

RACE AND ETHNIC DIVERSITY ● PHYSICAL DISABILITY ●

DIFFERENCES

Children are not born with prejudices – they learn them. This is one of the most important things to keep in mind if your children start asking questions about racial or religious differences, disabilities, or different ways of life, such as vegetarianism. The basis of your answers to all questions about differences should always be that everyone is the same inside and that external differences are nothing to be afraid of. Answering your children's questions about race or disability presents you with opportunities to teach tolerance and acceptance.

Judging a person by the way he looks or the food she eats is wrong, and you should discourage your child from thinking that way. Children have an innate sense of justice and fair play. Build on it; don't undermine or destroy it by allowing stereotypical views to take hold.

Do you eat meat?

Why is it rude to stare?

What's a vegetarian?

LEARNING DIFFICULTIES ● VEGETARIANISM ● ANIMAL WELFARE ●

Q Why isn't my skin brown?

- *Why is his skin a different color from mine?*

- *Why is her hair so curly?* ● *Why does Ben wear a little black cap?*

- *Why doesn't Akasi eat sausage?* ● *What does "racism" mean?*

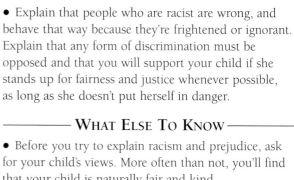

Racial prejudice in children is always the result of attitudes picked up at home and gleaned from their peer group – without these outside influences, children are not prejudiced. That isn't to say they don't notice differences, and when they ask questions about their observations it is important that you don't over-react; as ever, honest, factual answers are the key.

WHAT'S BEHIND THIS QUESTION

Children don't worry about racial differences by dress or skin color until they are programmed to do so by adults. Watch a mixed group of four- to five-year-olds playing and you'll see quite clearly that they regard each other as equals. Questions about racial differences may occur innocently from simple comparisons, but your child may start asking questions because she has heard others – children as well as adults – making racist remarks about people from backgrounds different from her own. This is a danger signal and needs to be treated accordingly. However, thoughtful older children may also pick up on problems caused by racism in the wider world – ethnic violence or cases of racial discrimination – reported on the news. Even though you may have brought up your child to be open and tolerant, she will need to understand that some people have bigoted ideas and she will need strength to counter them.

GUIDELINES FOR YOUR ANSWERS

- Try to always explore the point of view of people who seem different because of appearance or custom. Encourage your child to accept all differences as normal variations, not as signs of inferiority or superiority.

- Explain that people who are racist are wrong, and behave that way because they're frightened or ignorant. Explain that any form of discrimination must be opposed and that you will support your child if she stands up for fairness and justice whenever possible, as long as she doesn't put herself in danger.

WHAT ELSE TO KNOW

- Before you try to explain racism and prejudice, ask for your child's views. More often than not, you'll find that your child is naturally fair and kind.
- Don't ever encourage prejudice in your child by criticizing or making fun of other groups because of race, religion, dress, or skin color. If you have prejudices, spare your child. She is naturally impervious to suggestions of superiority or inferiority; don't encourage them in word or action.
- Under six, children are only interested in gender differences; other differences don't bother them.

Other things you may be asked...

- *Why do people hate someone who looks different?*
- *Why do other kids call Abdul bad names?*
- *What should I do if they call me bad names?*
- *Why does Sabiha wear different clothes than me?*

See also *What is religion? p. 46* ● *Why can't she walk? p. 70* ● *What's a bully? p. 82*

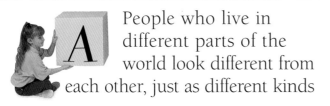

People who live in different parts of the world look different from each other, just as different kinds of birds do. But we're all people, whatever we look like.

People from different parts of the world often wear different kinds of clothes. There are so many different kinds of people living all over the Earth, whether it's cold or steamy hot, and they wear clothes to suit where they live. Even if people move somewhere else, they like to honor their past by wearing the things they're used to.

Some people are frightened of others who don't look or talk the same. When people are frightened they sometimes think things that aren't true. We're all human beings and we came from the same beginnings, even though people from Asia, Africa, Europe, and the Americas look different from one another now.

We're all the same human family and we should accept people for what they are, not what they look like. Some ignorant people try to show they're better than others by ganging up on them, or trying to keep them from getting good jobs and homes. It's good to stick up for Akasi – if someone calls him names, tell them not to, then tell your teacher or me.

When people are frightened they often become aggressive. They make fun of people who look different to make themselves feel more important. They may even use violence to try to prove that different people are inferior. But of course this isn't true; just because you won an argument doesn't make you superior to the person who lost. Some people will even fight wars because they think other people are inferior and must be suppressed. This is NEVER right. No one has the right to injure anyone else, let alone kill them. Always suspect someone who thinks like that and talk it over with us.

If people start saying bad things to you, try not to react – walk away. They're doing it because they are ignorant. If you see other people being bullied because of their ideas or appearances, try to stop it unless you're likely to be harmed yourself. Always tell Dad or Mom and we'll try to help you figure it out. No matter what a person wears, eats, or looks like, everyone in the world is equal and we all have the same human rights.

Q Why can't she walk?

- *Why does he look funny?* ● *Why can't he talk right?*
- *Why is she in a wheelchair?* ● *Why is she all twisted?*
- *Will she get better?* ● *Will I always be like this?*

Young children recognize the differences between people and will articulate this. But as with their comments about people from different ethnic backgrounds, it doesn't mean they are prejudiced or disgusted about disability; they will only become so if you fail to answer their questions about disabled people factually and sympathetically.

WHAT'S BEHIND THIS QUESTION

Your child isn't uncomfortable about people with disabilities in the way that some adults are. Your child may stare because he is curious, unlike the adult response to disabled people, which is often to look embarrassed or even repelled. Your child is really only interested in differences from himself, how they came about, if they could happen to him, and whether they are permanent. Equally, if your child is disabled, he is just as likely to ask questions about other people with different disabilities. Be reassuring on all these counts. Always stress that disabled people have the same rights as everyone else; they just happen to have a disability that makes their life more complicated than that of able-bodied people. Make it clear that enormous strength is required to overcome this.

GUIDELINES FOR YOUR ANSWERS

● Even if you feel embarrassment, try not to show it, but give honest answers. You can explain that many types of disability occur as a result of accidents to the unborn fetus or during birth. This information is reassuring for an able-bodied child because he'll know he got through those vulnerable times unscathed.

● Most disabilities are permanent, but with proper education and understanding, all disabled people can be helped to reach their full potential. Special features added to their homes, special transportation and equipment can also help.
● Encourage your child to ask disabled people if they need help and to give it if requested.

WHAT ELSE TO KNOW

● You and your children should always make full eye contact with disabled people while talking to them.
● You could help your child to develop caring and nurturing instincts by taking him to visit disabled children in a hospital, or to help in taking disabled people on an outing, such as a picnic or to the movies.
● Where appropriate support is available, disabled children are increasingly educated in ordinary schools, in regular classes. If your school has a mainstream policy, count yourself lucky. Get the advice of the teacher assigned to coordinate special educational needs in helping to answer your children's questions about disabled people.
● It's important for your child to understand that physical defects do *not* signify a slow mind or low intelligence and, like everyone else, disabled people have feelings that must be respected.
● It is equally important to encourage understanding of people with learning disabilities. Explain to your child that these people may experience life from a different perspective, but they are not inferior in any way.

Other things you may be asked...

■ *Was she born like that?*
■ *Why is it rude to stare?*
■ *Is she the same as me inside?*
■ *Should I help anyone with a white stick?*
■ *Why can't Grandma hear what I'm saying?*

See also *Where did I come from? p. 12* ● *Why isn't my skin brown? p. 68* ● *What's a bully? p. 82*

A She's not sick – she just needs help to do things. Sometimes something happens when babies are growing in their Mommies' tummies so they don't grow quite like other babies. Why don't you say "hello?"

A People with disabilities can't always do all the things other people can, so sometimes people think they need help. If you ask someone if they need help, remember that they think and feel just like you do – it's only their body that's different. They may need your help to do things, or they may just want to play with you. You should never make fun of a person who has disabilities – it's cruel.

A His body is bent because he probably couldn't breathe properly when he was being born so his brain didn't get enough oxygen. This sometimes stops the brain from giving the right signals to the muscles. It's not his fault and sometimes it must be very uncomfortable, but he will learn to do lots of things on his own, even if he seems to be struggling at the moment, and he goes to school just like you do. People with disabilities aren't different from us inside, although they sometimes need extra help to do everyday things that you and I might not have to think about.

A Disabled people are different from you in one of two small ways – either they can't do some things the way you can, or they don't think quite the same way that you do. Most disabled people overcome their disabilities and lead happy lives – including getting married and having children. Just because a person looks or talks differently from you, you must never make fun of them – teasing is just another form of bullying. Always remember that disabled people have the same rights as everyone else. When you talk to a disabled person always look at them; don't turn away. But everyone has the right to privacy, so people shouldn't keep snooping on them to make sure they're all right. Although able-bodied people have a responsibility to care for them, disabled people have the right to refuse help without causing resentment.

Q Do I have to eat meat?

- *Why do we eat meat?* • *Why do we make animals suffer for us?*
- *Do we have to eat animals to be healthy?*
- *Why do some people not eat meat?* • *What's a vegetarian?*

Your children may become aware of animal welfare issues surprisingly young, as films and television programs for children focus on them more and more. It doesn't take children long to make the link between the lamb in the field and the roast in the oven, and this could trigger a resistance to meat-eating.

WHAT'S BEHIND THIS QUESTION

Children are much more sensitive about animal suffering than many adults. Their sympathy for the pain animals might suffer at our hands is not tainted by adult justifications, such as "meat is good to eat," "animals aren't thinking beings, as we are," "animals don't feel as we do," "animal skins have been used to keep humans warm ever since man could hunt." Children focus solely on the possibility of pain, and, in a very humane way, equate animals to people, with the same rights as we have. It's an innocent approach and very clear and straightforward. It's also legitimate and should be taken seriously. It's not sentimental; it's about being fair and just to all living things.

GUIDELINES FOR YOUR ANSWERS

- You can't preach tolerance, kindness, and compassion to your children and then expect them to accept cruelty in any form to animals. Try to welcome such a sense of fairness and encourage it in them.
- Society's thinking is changing about animal welfare and animal rights are something everyone should think about and respect. Animals kept as pets deserve special

treatment because they mean a great deal to their owners. Children learn about love for others through loving and caring for pets, and no one would want to interfere with that. So respect your child's wishes if, as an owner of pets, she makes the connection between animals and food, and prefers not to eat meat.

- Be accommodating and accepting. Don't make fun of your child for caring about animals and not wanting to eat them. You'll be letting your child down, and she won't seek your help in future.

WHAT ELSE TO KNOW

- Very young children who refuse meat are unlikely to be doing it because they have realized it came from a live animal. At this age food preferences have far more to do with changing taste and experimentation. It may also come from a knowledge that mealtimes can provide an opportunity to assert individuality.
- Be reassured that children can eat a fully vegetarian diet and be healthy, though they may need vitamin supplements, particularly from the B group, and especially B_{12}, which has no direct plant source.
- Support your child's decision to become a vegetarian by reading as much as you can about it and making sure your child has a very wide diet of vegetarian foods.
- Vegetarians have to eat very large quantities to get all essential nutrients from plant sources alone. If you are a vegetarian yourself, be alert to this; it may be quite difficult for a small child to ingest the necessary bulk required to get enough nourishment. Think of your child before your vegetarian ethos.

Other things you may be asked...

- *Can children be vegetarians?*
- *Why do we kill animals to eat them?*
- *Do animals feel pain when they die?*
- *How do they kill animals for meat?*

See also *What happens when you die? p. 40* • *What is religion? p. 46*

A It's good for you to eat a little bit of meat or fish, because even a small piece has the goodness of lots of vegetables, and it's easier to eat! But we'll only have it once or twice a week and you can have cheese or eggs instead.

A You don't have to eat red meat if you really don't want to but it would be good for you to eat some white meat, like chicken, turkey, or fish. Yes, you can have your fish as fish sticks if you like. And I can make a special stew with tofu, with lots of vegetables. The less meat you eat the more vegetables and fruit you need to eat to stay healthy, so I'd like you to eat as many kinds as possible.

A A vegetarian is someone who doesn't eat any meat at all, even chicken, turkey, or fish. People are vegetarians for many reasons. Some believe it is wrong to kill animals at all, and don't think it's right for animals to suffer just to feed humans, especially as animals sometimes live in very cramped conditions. Other people think growing crops just to feed animals that are killed for food is wrong when there are so many people in the world who haven't got enough to eat – they think the land should be used for crops to feed people instead.

A Human beings are mostly "omnivorous," which means we eat both animal and vegetable foods. Our bodies evolved to be able to use food from animal and vegetable sources. Humans have teeth to tear and chew meat and complicated chemicals called enzymes in our intestines to release the protein in meat, which is a very efficient food: small quantities contain lots of protein and amino acids. But people need to eat lots more vegetables and fruit as well to stay healthy.

We don't know for sure what happens to animals when they die, but we do know that all pain and suffering stops. The animals we eat are killed as painlessly as possible, but if you don't eat meat because you don't think animals should suffer at all, I will respect your wishes. I can easily get you vegetarian foods at the supermarket. Why don't you come with me, then you can choose, and we'll find out what you really like and learn to cook it together.

QUESTIONS ABOUT

What's
a bully?

Will all
strangers
hurt me?

Does
AIDS
hurt?

Why do
people
smoke?

Do I
have to
kiss him?

Why can't
I talk to
strangers?

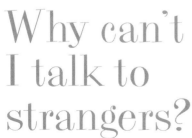

Can I hit
him back?

CHILD PROTECTION ● BULLYING ● VIOLENCE AND WAR

SAFETY & HEALTH

It is undoubtedly true that today's parents generally fear for their children's safety in ways that may never have occurred to an older generation. While the world may be no more dangerous than it was, say fifty years ago, people are now more aware of the dangers to which children could be exposed. Knowledge of child abuse, both physical and sexual, is widespread; the damage to health from drugs, smoking and alcohol is widely publicized, and the spread of AIDS – a disease that by its very nature creates fear and uncertainty – is constantly reiterated by the media. No wonder that you may feel overprotective toward your children and want to shield them from these constant dangers. Children need to believe that they can come to you about anything and that you'll always take them seriously. You can help build this trust by listening to their questions, believing what they say, and being ready to respond at once. Given enough accurate information to protect themselves, your children will grow up with a sense of proportion about all areas of personal safety and health.

Why did you shout at me?

Why do people get drunk?

Q Why can't I talk to strangers?

- *Why shouldn't I take a present from someone I don't know?*
- *Why can't I ride home in a stranger's car?*
- *Where can I go to get away from someone I don't know?*

Fear for the safety of your children is an unfortunate fact of modern life. However, it is possible to equip them with strategies to combat the unwelcome attentions of strangers. These will give you peace of mind, so that their movements don't have to be unnaturally restricted as they get older.

WHAT'S BEHIND THIS QUESTION

Children may be confused by the idea that what appears to be kindness may be harmful to them. After all, you teach them that kindness is good, so they naturally interpret anyone's kindness that way. In fact, you have to warn your child about strangers before they're old enough to ask questions, and you have to go on encouraging them not to trust people they don't know. Even when my sons were in their late teens I used to exhort them not to speak to strangers whenever they went to the city. To a child, anyone offering candy or toys, or the promise of an exciting treat like a visit to an amusement park, is attractive, and someone who will save them a walk home is a godsend, so their questions will reflect their bewilderment at the contrary messages they are getting about adult behavior.

GUIDELINES FOR YOUR ANSWERS

- Because of children's innate trust of kind adults, they need to be taught one of life's tough lessons – that things may be more sinister than they seem. But it's important to strike a balance in what you say. You want to protect your children and give them enough information to protect themselves, but you don't want them to lose their friendliness and become totally mistrusting of everyone. That would be unfair to your children, but their safety is paramount. It's not easy.

- The aim should be to educate your child in a nonalarmist way to steer clear of strangers whatever the inducements, so that it becomes part of normal life – a given, nonnegotiable fact, like not touching electric outlets or not handling sharp knives.

WHAT ELSE TO KNOW

- Children need very clear instructions on how to act in certain circumstances. Draw up a checklist like a drill and repeat it endlessly until your child knows it by heart. Make it easy to remember by including rhymes and rhythms. Make sure your child learns his address and telephone number – and his full name – as early as possible, and include the telephone number of a children's Helpline in your area, if one exists.

- As a parent it is a good idea always to know where your child is. This may seem obvious, but it is all too easy to be concentrating on something else and then turn around to find your child has wandered out of sight. At the same time, you probably don't want to completely restrict an older child's movements. Make it clear from the beginning that the rule is that your child can go out if he is always with friends and that they all know the "drill" that you have been teaching your own child. Encourage your child to take responsibility for knowing exactly when he is expected home and always to telephone you if there is a change of plan.

- Encourage a bit of assertiveness so that your child won't be afraid to stand his ground. Play-act some possible situations with your child, too, to make sure he is aware of what might happen.

Other things you may be asked...

- *Will all strangers hurt me?*
- *What do I do if someone talks to me?*
- *What do I do if someone gives me candy?*
- *What do I do if someone offers me a ride in their car?*

See also *Why does his Mom shout at him? p. 80* • *What does violence mean? p. 84*

A I don't like you speaking to people you don't know because they might not be kind to you. Giving you candy doesn't mean they're kind, and it doesn't mean they care about you. Never get into a car or go for a walk with anyone, even a child, without asking Mommy or Daddy first.

A If a stranger tries to talk to you, stay away. Go into the nearest restaurant or store, and say "Please help me, I'm scared." If there's no store, look for a woman who looks like she has children. Stay where there are people.

A You must never speak to strangers or go near them. NEVER walk in the street alone. Even if it's just a little way, always go with friends – there's safety in numbers. NEVER go out into the street after dark, even with friends. Don't let them speak to strangers, either – if one of them does or gets into a stranger's car, run straight home and tell us. If you're left on your own, even if you know the way home, get a grown-up you know to call us and one of us will pick you up. If you're ever frightened or lost, look for a police officer or go into a nearby business. Remember to say your name, address, and phone number.

A A few people, mainly men, like hurting children. You must try to stay away from them because they're stronger than you are. Being with a group of friends is a safeguard, but if it's dark and you're taking a short cut home through the alley, then even a crowd of friends might not be able to help you. So always walk in wide, well-lit streets, at the outside edge of the pavement. Walk purposefully, keep your head up, swing your arms, and carry something like a sports bag. Strangers hardly ever approach anyone walking like that. If a stranger ever gets hold of you, shout to your friends to get help quickly or to tell us or another grown-up they trust right away. Don't ever be rude to a stranger, and never pick a fight. If you get lost, you should try to find a police officer or a meter maid, or go into a nearby restaurant or store. Ask if you can borrow the phone to contact us by calling collect. We could give you a phone card as well.

Q Do I have to let him kiss me?

- *Do I have to sit on his knee?* ● *Is keeping secrets ever wrong?*
- *Is it ever right for someone to touch me down there?*
- *Are uncles/grandfathers always right?*

The possibility of sexual abuse of your child is something most parents prefer not to think about. But it does happen, and sadly the perpetrators are often people very close to the abused child – frequently, in the same family. Abused children often feel doubly guilty if they reveal their abuse, so their questions may contain hidden clues.

——— WHAT'S BEHIND THIS QUESTION ———

The sort of questions I have given above are typical danger signs of sexual abuse, one of the most pernicious ways in which children can be exploited. Unfortunately, it often involves someone close to the child, who can create an emotional smokescreen based on "special secrets" combined with veiled threats. Many children are afraid of adults for quite innocuous reasons, but a child who is being abused often senses that something is really wrong, particularly if she is specifically being asked to keep something secret from her parents. Children who have been sworn to secrecy may be too frightened to speak out, so be alert to questions that may signal that

someone is taking advantage of your child's innocence. Be sensitive to other signs, such as the child becoming withdrawn, refusing to eat, showing reluctance to visit a particular relative, or having nightmares.

——— GUIDELINES FOR YOUR ANSWERS ———

- Children need to know that they can come to you about anything and you'll take them seriously. I get many letters from abused children who are scared to tell their parents because they feel they won't be believed.
- You need to be very calm and prepared for gentle probing to discover what has triggered the question. Make it clear that your child can tell you anything, even very big secrets, and reassure her that you'll protect her.

——— WHAT ELSE TO KNOW ———

- Most child sexual abuse is done by someone the child knows and trusts. This can be a shock, but you owe it to your child to believe her – avoid automatically dismissing what she tells you as fantasy or over-reaction – or you may unwittingly perpetuate the abuse.
- Even when you point out that what the person has been doing is bad, your child may feel she can't tell on him, because she doesn't want him to suffer.
- All abused children think they're somehow to blame. Take time to assure your child that it's not her fault and she won't get into any trouble if she's truthful.
- If it becomes clear that the abuser is the child's parent, then his or her partner must get help. The shame and grief this causes is terrible, but the prime responsibility must be to protect the child, not the abuser.

Other things you may be asked...

- *Do I have to sleep in the same room as him?*
- *Do I always have to do what a grown-up tells me?*
- *Do I have to obey older boys and girls?*
- *Will I go to prison if I tell someone's secret?*

See also *What is sex? p. 18* ● *Why can't I talk to strangers? p. 76*

A You never have to kiss or hug anyone if you don't want to. It's NEVER right for someone to touch your private places, so you must always say "no" and tell me. You never have to keep secrets from Mommy if anyone tells you to, even if they say something bad will happen. Come and tell me right away and I'll make sure nothing bad happens.

FOR AGES 2–6

A No one who cares for you will ask you to do something wrong or hurtful. You should do as you're asked in the classroom but not if a teacher wants you to do something alone with him or her that seems odd. You don't have to do anything involving touching or kissing that anyone else tells you to do. Just say "I don't want to do that," or "I don't want to play that game," or "I have to go home now." If someone asks you to keep a secret about something, it usually means that they know Mommy would be angry at them if she found out. It's wrong to ask you not to tell. You can share your secrets, especially if they make you unhappy. If someone tells you you'll go to prison or go to hell if you tell on them, they're lying. They just say it to make you frightened. Don't worry, Mommy will help you and you'll never be blamed. I will protect you from harm, and you can always trust me.

FOR AGES 6–8

A Some grown-ups like doing sexy things to children, boys and girls. They're BAD and it's very wrong because it's a mean kind of bullying. They think they can make you do things because they're stronger and older than you are. That is never right.

It's against the law for anyone to do anything sexual to you against your will – that's called rape – and it's also against the law to have sex with anyone who's under the age of 16. If anyone tries to touch you in a sexual way, or wants you to touch them, even if it is someone in our family, tell them what I've told you. You don't ever have to do it, even if they offer you big treats. If you think that anyone is especially interested in you and might try to be sexual, tell Mom right away and I'll make sure that you're never with them on your own. Of course you don't have to share a bed when you go to your cousin's house. You don't have to do what he says just because he's older than you. I'll tell his parents you can't go there any more.

Sometimes children blame themselves and think it's all their fault if horrible things happen to them, but you must remember that it's never a child's fault if an older boy or girl or a grown-up tries to do something bad like this.

FOR AGES 8–11

Q Why does his Mom shout at him?

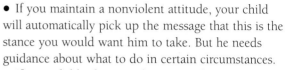

- *Why do you have to shout at me?* ● *Is it ever right to hit someone?*
- *Why are you always angry with me?* ● *Why did you hit me?*
- *Why has Jamie got marks all over his legs and arms?*

Everyone has moments of stress that may result in shouting at or even hitting a child for a minor misdemeanor. Usually it passes, parents feel guilty, there are apologies all around, and it doesn't happen again. But anything more than a rare light slap becomes abuse and everyone involved needs help.

- If you maintain a nonviolent attitude, your child will automatically pick up the message that this is the stance you would want him to take. But he needs guidance about what to do in certain circumstances.
- If your child asks you why you are being constantly aggressive or hurtful, take it seriously, and look at yourself critically. You need to be able to answer that question yourself as well.

—— WHAT ELSE TO KNOW ——

Shouting aggressively is as much a form of abuse as hitting. If you constantly shout at a child, he won't know how to respond to normal levels of conversation. Regularly running him down, laughing at him, threatening to withdraw your love or previously promised treats, are all forms of emotional abuse. In time, they could have a permanent effect on his self-esteem, so try to maintain a balance.

—— WHAT'S BEHIND THIS QUESTION ——

There are many kinds of abuse – even emotional abuse, which may not show any physical scars – but most children believe that what happens to them is the norm, which is why even battered and abused children cling to their parents. Once a child's world widens beyond the home, he can make comparisons and may begin to realize that his situation isn't acceptable. Many children are afraid of adults who abuse them, and make excuses for their injuries – "I fell down," "I walked into a door." They may think, with some justification, that things will be worse for them if they reveal the abuse they are suffering. Another child, however, who sees the evidence of physical abuse, may speak out, especially if he sees a child being chastised for no apparent reason. A child who suffers verbal abuse at home but whose teachers speak gently to him will begin to wonder why others don't too, even if he's used to being shouted at all the time.

—— GUIDELINES FOR YOUR ANSWERS ——

- Physical punishment, violence, and constant verbal abuse all have a brutalizing effect on children, and no one decides to bring up children in that way.

Other things you may be asked...

- *What's a battered child?*
- *What do I do if a grown-up hits me?*
- *Should I tell someone if Jerry gets bruises again?*
- *Why are you always laughing at me?*

See also *Do I have to let him kiss me? p. 78* ● *What's a bully? p. 82* ● *What does violence mean? p. 84*

A This question is unlikely to be asked by children under four, although they may be frightened by seeing, especially receiving, verbal or physical abuse. If a young child asks this question, base your answers on the 4–6 age group.

A I don't know why she shouts at him, but whatever the reason, it must make him sad. Perhaps her mother shouted at her and she thinks it's what parents do. I sometimes lose my temper with you, too, because I get angry too easily when I'm very busy, but that's not an excuse. I love you very much and I don't like shouting at you so I will try not to. Tell me if I do it again. Shouting and hitting are both wrong; there are other ways to show you're angry, like using quiet words.

A People sometimes hit other people because they're angry or frightened. It's always wrong. No argument can be settled by a fight – it's best to try to talk it through. And if people won't talk, we should walk away. Jerry's got lots of bruises, hasn't he? A bruise shows where something has bumped hard against the skin. He might have gotten them falling downstairs like he says, but if they're all over his body, there's probably another reason. If he comes into school with bruises next week, tell me and I'll talk to the teacher. By telling me, you might be able to stop Jerry from being hurt anymore.

A Sometimes it's very difficult to avoid being hit or hitting someone back. If another child hits you, tell him to stop and say if he hits you again, you'll hit him back. This will stop most people. But only hit him yourself if he hits you again, and it's the only way to get away; then run and tell me or Dad or your teacher. We'll deal with it quietly, don't worry. But if a grown-up hits you – even if it's someone we know very well, even in our family, you must tell me right away, and I'll take care of it. Some grown-ups get very angry inside when life is difficult for them and they take it out on children by hitting them, or not giving them enough to eat or things like that. A battered child is a baby or little child who has been hurt a lot by his parents. Often the parents believe they love the baby really, but they can't cope with taking care of it and treat it badly. Hurting a child is never right. Sometimes the baby is placed in a foster home while the parents are helped to learn how to care for their baby with love.

Q What's a bully?

- *Why does David keeps hitting Andrew?* • *What's bullying?*
- *Why does he take my lunch money?* • *Can I hit him back?*
- *Will you stop those kids from picking on me?*

Bullying is one of the most insidious problems within schools – and it can exist in any school, in any community, among any children. Vigilant teachers in a school with a positive policy on bullying will want to nip it in the bud, so if your child's questions hint at bullying, take it to your school's principal immediately.

WHAT'S BEHIND THIS QUESTION

Questions about bullying are usually asked because your child has seen it at school or depicted on TV, but be on the lookout for signs of it happening to your own child. Sometimes you may have to be something of a sleuth. We only discovered one of our sons was being bullied because he kept asking for money – a gang of bullies at school was demanding money from him. Most children have a natural sense of fair play and hate to see classmates victimized, so they could question you about that, too.

GUIDELINES FOR YOUR ANSWERS

- Bullying is always wrong and must be stopped. Persuade your child of this whatever way you can. She will find it easier to tell you about bullying if she is clear about this basic belief.

- Boys, particularly, are conscious of the ridiculous code that they mustn't tell on bullies, even if they are the victims. Convince your children that this code is wrong and they must seek help if bullied.
- You may wonder whether your child should retaliate if faced with bullying. Before he turned nine, I used to tell my son to give the bully one warning and then hit back, but a child shouldn't do this if faced with several others. A child can ask a trusted older child to help deal with bullies, but you should always report bullying to the school, even if it is happening outside the school premises, and ask for the staff's help to discipline bullies, in a discreet way so as to protect your child.
- Girls are just as capable of bullying as boys, and very often it takes the form of a cruel whispering campaign, or deliberately excluding a child from a group of friends. If prolonged, this can be just as wounding as physical violence and should be taken seriously.

WHAT ELSE TO KNOW

- Children aren't born bullies but often learn a pattern of selfishness, victimization, and bullying from adults in their own homes. This may be due to excessive strictness from authoritarian parents or arise in a home that is disorganized, where a child is neglected.
- Bullying is a child's response to pain, discomfort, and lack of love, and can be part of general behavior disorders like stealing, lying, and truancy. While bullying can never be condoned, these children need help to change their pattern of behavior.

Other things you may be asked...

- *Why does that girl keep hitting me?*
- *Why do people bully?*
- *What can I do if someone picks on me?*
- *Will he hit me if I tell the teacher?*
- *How can I stop them hitting him?*

See also *Why can't I make friends? p. 62* • *Why do I have to go to school? p. 64*

A If Nicky hurts you again at school tell me and I'll speak to the teacher for you. Lots of people are called names; I was called Dumbo because I had big ears, but it's just silly, so try to ignore it.

A No one should hit anyone else, so if Peter punches you some more, tell him you'll tell the teacher. You must tell the teacher and me because Peter could hurt a lot of other people, too. He's hitting people because he's very unhappy about something, so he feels scared and lashes out. If we tell your teacher maybe we can all help him feel better about things.

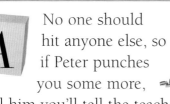

A You know Mommy and Daddy don't approve of violence – punching and hitting – but bullies are bad; they must be stopped. So this is what you do next time: give the bully one warning and say if he attacks you again you'll hit him back, then go and tell your teacher what happened. Tell me, too, as soon as possible. And if he does hit you again, give him one big swipe, and then quickly go and tell your teacher. Don't try to hit back if there's more than one bully. Don't worry, your teacher knows how to deal with bullies, so I promise nothing bad will happen if you tell.

A Bullying is always wrong and bullies mustn't be allowed to get away with it. Picking on someone for any reason is never right. But that girl who is picking on you is probably very unhappy underneath, for some reason. Bullying is a way of pretending she isn't unhappy. But we have to think of how to stop her and then maybe someone will be able to find out why she's doing it. It isn't a good idea to try to hit back more than once – this will just lead to a fight, which bullies like. The best thing is to tell your teacher about it – ask a friend to come with you for moral support. If you have an older friend, she'll help if you tell her about it. But tell me, too, because I won't let bullies victimize you. I'll go to the school and we'll work out with the teachers how to stop these bullies in a very discreet way.

Q What does violence mean?

- *Why are people violent?* • *What's a mugger?*

- *Why do people blow things up with bombs?*

- *When people throw bricks through windows, is that violent?*

Children are exposed to many violent images nowadays, and learn about violent situations from television news and newspapers, so their reactions and questions may be confused. Striking a balance between your own desire to protect your children and keep them out of trouble, and the realities of war and terrorism is a difficult one for parents.

WHAT'S BEHIND THIS QUESTION

Over the age of four, children are old enough to know that violence – mental or physical – is undesirable, even evil, and out of a sense of fairness will want some guidelines about how to recognize it, and how to act when they meet it. Out of a sense of injustice they may want to intervene precipitately but, as with bullying (p. 82), you'll have to coach them about when that's proper or safe and when to hang back, even though their instincts are laudable. Children are also disturbed and confused by street and terrorist violence, and by the destructive images of war that they see every day in newspapers and on television (fictional as well as factual) and whose causes are inexplicable to them.

GUIDELINES FOR YOUR ANSWERS

• To answer questions about violence sincerely you'll have to believe that violence is never justifiable, with the possible exception of some wars – though your child won't be able to understand this until they're eight or nine. Up to that age you won't go wrong if you condemn violence in all its guises as an inappropriate way to solve problems or behave at any time.

• Violent adults breed violent children; we shouldn't pass on that legacy to a new young generation.
• Of course, for your child's own safety you will have to teach that intervention in violence is dangerous to them, and they must avoid it.

WHAT ELSE TO KNOW

Your child is bound to meet violence sooner or later. I decided that much as I hated violence I could not go on forever teaching pacifism to my children, as they could come to serious harm if they thought they could rely solely on the intelligence of others to resolve arguments peaceably. So I taught them the "retaliate once and run" technique so that they would feel they had some control in unpleasant circumstances.

If you let your children watch TV on their own, be aware that violent images can appear at any time.

Other things you may be asked...

- *Is being angry/rude/mean the same as being violent?*
- *Is violence ever right?*
- *Is what happened in Oklahoma City violent?*
- *When people go on a march, is that violent?*
- *What do I do if I see someone hurting my friends?*

See also *Why isn't my skin brown? p. 68* • *Why does his Mom shout at him? p. 80* • *What's a bully? p. 82*

Children under four years old are unlikely to ask this question, although they are likely to notice and be alarmed by violent behavior. If a mature 3½-year-old asks you about violence, base your answer on the 4–6 age group.

A Violence means really hurting or injuring someone because you don't agree with them or don't like them. You feel so mad you want to strike out and try to make them feel pain. It's never right. We can feel angry with someone but that doesn't ever give us the right to hurt them. In some places people plant bombs because they hate one another so much. Killing is the worst kind of violence and if they're caught, killers go to prison, sometimes for the rest of their lives.

A There are people who feel that they want to hurt people different from them by punishing them with violence. If you see someone being violent, don't get involved yourself, but get an adult to intervene. Sometimes people think violence is the only response, especially if they have suffered violence themselves. That's why some people set off bombs – they think it's the only way to get what they want. Regardless of the reasons, it's never right to be violent. When whole countries or different people in the same country are aggressive to each other it can lead to wars. Politicians try to stop wars by finding ways of solving the basic problem.

A People of different races or religions sometimes hate one another enough to hurt each other or frighten people in their homes. If one kind of people does that to other people with different skin color or from another country, it's racial violence. This is always wrong – everyone has the right to live peacefully together, regardless of race, religion, or nationality. Sometimes if people who have different views get together, for instance at a rock concert or a street demonstration, they get angry and start fighting. But it's never right to use violence to force your point of view. A mugger is someone who uses violence to rob someone in the street. If you see someone being mugged or beaten up, don't intervene – you're too young – but hurry to find an adult to get the police.

Q What's alcohol?

- *Why is alcohol bad?* • *Why can't I have beer/wine?*
- *What's "drunk" mean?* • *Why do you always have wine at meals?*
- *What do I do if someone tries to make me have a drink?*

Alcohol is a drug, yet it is perfectly legal, so it is no wonder that children may be bewildered by the subject. There's plenty of publicity about the dangers of drinking and driving, and older children may be exposed to scenes involving drunks on television, so questions are sure to arise. You may need to think carefully about your own attitude toward drinking alcohol and how consistent you are.

WHAT'S BEHIND THIS QUESTION

For young children, the appeal of alcoholic drinks is a bit of a mystery, because they generally find the taste unpleasant. Older children who ask questions like these are trying to figure out why some things are all right for adults but not for them. It seems to them like a double standard, and they are right, so you've got to have your thoughts very clear and your answers prepared. Your child may also know someone who is suffering as a result of someone's drinking, so you need to be alert and be prepared to provide discreet help.

GUIDELINES FOR YOUR ANSWERS

- Alcohol is a poison, but it isn't illegal, and it is difficult to convince children of this when they see so many adults drinking. But it is worth noting that anyone could die of alcoholic poisoning if too much is consumed too quickly – for instance, half a bottle of whiskey in a couple of hours.
- The aim is to encourage your child to be sensible, moderate, and to take personal responsibility for sobriety when she is old enough to drink alcohol.
- Most parents are aware of worsening statistics on underage drinking and so may be tempted to be strict;

I don't think this works. On almost any question of discipline, an authoritarian approach has negative results.
- By the time your child is eight or nine you can start giving them basic information on the harmful effects of alcohol. Children of this age are generally very receptive to health arguments and they'll usually respond to calm and reasonable explanations.

WHAT ELSE TO KNOW

- I belong to the school of thought that believes anything that is banned automatically becomes very attractive to children. So candy and treats weren't banned in our house, nor was television, and nor was alcohol, but they were all carefully rationed.
- Even very young children may like the taste of some alcoholic drinks, but that's not a reason for giving it to them. Be aware that the alcoholic "soft drinks" taste pleasant but are very strong. Avoid them. However, if adults were drinking wine with a meal I would give any child who requested it a taste. Up to the age of 10 most children detest the taste and spit it out. After that some may enjoy wine diluted with a lot of water and by about 12 or 13 like half a glass of wine undiluted.
- Help them to learn by your example; a good habit to instill in them from the start is never to drink alcohol on an empty stomach, but only at mealtimes with other people. Always drink lots of water with it.
- Alcohol in small quantities taken with food is not unhealthy; some researchers believe that it actually confers extra years of life, so keep this long-term view in mind while teaching moderation.

Other things you may be asked...

- *How can you tell when someone is drunk?*
- *Why do people get drunk?*
- *Which drinks are strongest?*
- *Do you drink and drive?*

See also *Why is smoking bad for you? p. 88* • *What are drugs? p. 90*

Children under four are very unlikely to ask questions on this subject. However, they may be curious if you are drinking alcohol and the questions may arise from that. Adapt my answer for the 4–6 age group, if necessary.

A Alcohol is a chemical that is in some kinds of drinks like wine and beer, and gin and whiskey. When people drink it, it makes them feel relaxed and friendly. But if they take too much it's like a poison and makes people drunk, so they get out of control and feel sick and get a headache. But a little wine or beer isn't bad for most grown-ups at mealtimes.

A If people drink a lot of alcohol, they can become addicted to it, just like drugs or cigarettes. Drinking too much alcohol is very bad because it poisons the liver and if the liver is worn out you die. Drinking alcohol also means you can't drive safely, even though people sometimes think they can, and people who are drunk often cause car accidents. No, I've never been drunk like that but I've been a little bit tipsy. We have wine with dinner because it's safer to drink alcohol with food and it's relaxing.

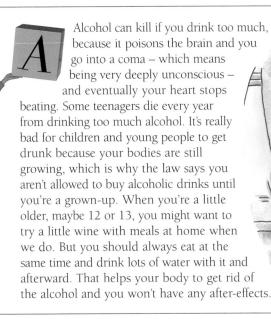

A Alcohol can kill if you drink too much, because it poisons the brain and you go into a coma – which means being very deeply unconscious – and eventually your heart stops beating. Some teenagers die every year from drinking too much alcohol. It's really bad for children and young people to get drunk because your bodies are still growing, which is why the law says you aren't allowed to buy alcoholic drinks until you're a grown-up. When you're a little older, maybe 12 or 13, you might want to try a little wine with meals at home when we do. But you should always eat at the same time and drink lots of water with it and afterward. That helps your body to get rid of the alcohol and you won't have any after-effects.

Q Why is smoking bad for you?

● *Why do people smoke?* ● *Why do you smoke?*

● *Why does Grandpa smoke a pipe?* ● *What does smoking feel like?*

● *Why don't you give up smoking?*

Although fewer people smoke regularly nowadays, and smoking is forbidden in many public places, children are still regularly in contact with people who smoke, and teenage smoking is rising. Yet children are taught early on that tobacco is a legal drug that is bad for you, so they are bound to ask questions about it, especially if either of their parents smokes as well.

WHAT'S BEHIND THIS QUESTION

The antismoking lobby is very well organized and your child will receive the message that smoking is bad for you from an early age. He will also notice that in spite of this, people still smoke. If a family member smokes as well, your child will soon make known his puzzlement at the conflicting signals.

GUIDELINES FOR YOUR ANSWERS

● Even if you are a smoker yourself, you owe it to your child to point out the dangers of smoking, both to your own health and to others who inhale your smoke secondhand as "passive smokers."

● Unlike the way you handle alcohol, you need to try and put across the message forcefully that it is better never to start smoking, however strong the pressure may be from your children's friends. Stress how difficult it is to give up once you become addicted.

● Children under the age of 10 are less likely to be pushed into smoking, but it is a good idea to prepare them for the heavy peer pressure that will undoubtedly happen to them in their early teens, when statistics show that smoking is, unfortunately, on the increase, particularly among girls.

WHAT ELSE TO KNOW

● Like alcohol, cigarettes are addictive drugs that happen to be legal. However, in the United States it is illegal for anyone to sell cigarettes to children under 18.

● When I told a seminar of 13- and 14-year-olds that smoking should be forbidden in schools, I was told that this would contravene a teenager's human right to act freely and smoke. This is the propaganda of the tobacco companies, but it can be countered with the argument that underlies other public safety laws such as speed limits on roads: that rights also involve responsibilities, and individual rights are overridden by the rights of everyone to safety and good health.

● A 1989 survey of 10,000 nine to 15-year-olds found that parental attitudes are important: children are less likely to smoke if parents are against smoking. A more recent survey found that the vast majority of boys and girls aged 11 said they didn't smoke and wouldn't, although smoking among high school seniors remained around 30 per cent.

Other things you may be asked...

■ *What do I do if someone tries to make me smoke a cigarette?*

■ *Why do so many people smoke if they know it's bad?*

■ *Why can't I buy cigarettes?*

■ *Why did Auntie Jean start smoking again?*

See also *What happens when you die? p. 40* ● *Why do some babies die? p. 42* ● *What's alcohol? p. 86*

Children under the age of four will rarely ask questions about smoking, but may be curious if they see someone smoking.

If a mature 3½-year-old raises the subject, base your answers on those given for children in the 4–6 age group.

FOR AGES 2–4

FOR AGES 2–4

A Smoking is always bad for you. It damages your heart and lungs, and it also hurts people around you. Smokers find it difficult to stop, so it's best never to start at all.

FOR AGES 4–6

A When people smoke, tar from the smoke gets inside their lungs and makes it difficult for them to breathe properly. This can take a long time, so some people who smoke believe it will never happen to them. But we know that smoking causes lung cancer and heart attacks, and lots of people die because of those two things. I used to smoke but I don't now. I stopped when you were in my tummy because smoking is bad for babies and children.

FOR AGES 6–8

A Smoking is never good for anyone. It damages the lungs so they get clogged up, and it causes lung diseases that make people very weak because they can't breathe properly. And it causes lung cancer which kills thousands of people all over the world every year. It also causes heart attacks because smoking makes people's veins and arteries tighten up, so every year it also causes thousands of deaths from heart disease.

If you possibly can, I'd like you never to start smoking because it's addictive. This means your body gets used to the drug called nicotine that is in tobacco. Nicotine makes you want it all the time, so it's hard to stop smoking. Luckily some people do manage to give up because they know it's so bad for them. And it's just as bad if you breathe in the smoke from someone else's cigarette – that's called "passive smoking."

Young people start smoking because they think it's grown up, but it isn't healthy. It's never "grown up" and "cool" to poison yourself. If any of your friends are smoking, just say, "No, thanks, I don't want to" and walk away. You can say you're allergic to smoke, which should stop them from pressuring you. Pay no attention if they tease or call you chicken, just go away and do something else. Remember that smoking makes their breath and clothes smell horrible and it'll make their teeth and fingers turn yellow.

FOR AGES 8–11

● *What are drugs? p. 90*

Q What are drugs?

- *What happens if you smoke pot or sniff glue?* • *What's grass?*
- *Why do people die from taking ecstasy?* • *What's "shooting up"?*
- *What's crack/cocaine?* • *How do I say no to drugs?*

All parents worry about whether their child will experiment with drugs, although few consider that this might be relevant to children under ten. But drugs may now be an issue even for this age group, so it is far better to answer questions about drugs accurately and straightforwardly than to duck the issue. Make sure your child will be prepared when faced with the reality later.

WHAT'S BEHIND THIS QUESTION

Whether we like it or not, drugs are now part of school culture. Taking drugs is seen by most young people as exciting and glamorous. It's also the subject of forceful peer pressure. Although children aren't generally exposed to drug-taking until they are at least 12 or 13, there is evidence that children as young as nine or 10 are dealing and taking drugs. While this is still comparatively rare, your child could be exposed to drug talk quite early, so with questions like these, your child may simply be looking for information, but equally she may be asking for help. Be proud of your child for asking, try to ascertain how prevalent drugs are at school, and report back discreetly to the teacher or principal.

GUIDELINES FOR YOUR ANSWERS

- You should try to prepare your child for exposure to drugs by giving specific advice on what to do and say to resist them. If possible, give this advice early enough to avoid her being caught unawares.
- What you say to your child should be honest but low-key, in order to give her an accurate picture of the dangers of taking drugs, without being alarmist.

- The greatest antidote to taking hard drugs is high self-esteem, so make sure you help your child feel that she is great, and that you love her, no matter what.

WHAT ELSE TO KNOW

- Marijuana is not addictive. On its own it probably does less harm than cigarettes, although many people smoke it with tobacco and there is evidence that heavy consumption can lead to memory loss. Smoking marijuana doesn't necessarily lead to hard drugs, so getting very upset about it is inappropriate. However, there is no getting away from the fact that it is illegal.
- Certain conditions make a child vulnerable to hard drugs: low self-esteem, being ignored or starved of affection; receiving overzealous discipline; or living in a disorganized home with drunken parents.
- The newer drugs of the dance culture, such as ecstasy, are dangerous because their effect is unpredictable. You may convince your 10-year-old they can lead to death, but sustaining that fear into her teens when she's exposed to them regularly will need careful handling.
- Sniffing solvents can be a problem even with young children. You should suspect solvent abuse if you find glue, lighter fuel, or correction fluid among your children's belongings, or if your child smells of the fluid. Solvent abuse can cause sudden death, so if you think your child has been sniffing solvents, call the doctor before you do anything else.
- Make sure your own consumption of alcohol or prescription drugs doesn't give your child a confusing, contradictory example of double standards.

Other things you may be asked...

- *Is dope bad for you?*
- *Can you die from taking LSD?*
- *What does "addiction/hooked" mean?*
- *How do you die from taking heroin?*

See also *What happens when you die? p. 40* • *Why is smoking bad for you? p. 88* • *What is AIDS? p. 92*

Children under six are unlikely to ask questions about drugs or drug-taking unless they hear someone else mention the subject. If a mature 4–6-year-old asks about drugs, use my answer for the 6–8 age group, adapting it according to your child's level of understanding.

A Hard drugs are the ones that are habit-forming – you become addicted or "hooked" on them – which means you need to take them often and it's very difficult to stop. Addicts don't want to eat and you become very thin and sick. Hard drugs can eventually kill you because they're poison and they can make you go into a coma and stop breathing. Hard drugs are cocaine and heroin, and crack – which is smokable cocaine. Some drugs are not addictive but, apart from marijuana, they can be very dangerous because they affect people in different ways, but no one knows in advance how they're going to react. Even the first pill can kill people or make them so sick that they never recover. Drugs like ecstasy, LSD, and "magic mushrooms" can all do that so its best not to try them. Children have died the first time they've sniffed glue or other things like cleaning fluid. This is because they all have a chemical in them that affects the brain and makes you do and think stupid things. Sometimes these drugs can be like a terrible nightmare that never goes away – that's called a bad trip. Some people never recover from a bad trip.

A "Grass" is marijuana. There are lots of other names for it like pot, mary jane, hash, or weed. Marijuana is usually smoked like a cigarette. People who smoke it now and then don't usually go on to hard drugs. It doesn't do you much harm unless you smoke it regularly, but it can damage the lungs because people tend to inhale it more deeply than cigarette smoke, and it can affect your memory. People smoke pot because it makes them feel giggly and floaty, but it is against the law. When you're older and start going to clubs, you might get offered pills like ecstasy. These are dangerous because you don't know how badly they will affect you. The best thing is just to say "No, thanks" and walk away so the person trying to make you take one can't keep nagging you about it. Tell him you don't need that kind of help to have a good time. People take hard drugs because they feel unhappy, depressed, or lonely, or think that nobody loves them. But you know that you're terrific, and we think that, too.

Q What is AIDS?

- *What's HIV?* ● *How do you get AIDS?* ● *Can anyone get AIDS?*
- *Does AIDS make you very ill?* ● *Does AIDS hurt?*
- *Do children get AIDS?* ● *Do all people with AIDS die?*

Information about HIV and AIDS must be an integral part of sex education for all children. Times have changed immeasurably from when the only reason for "safe sex" was to avoid unwanted pregnancies, so it is literally a matter of life and death to provide accurate and honest answers about AIDS, however uncomfortable it may be.

WHAT'S BEHIND THIS QUESTION

AIDS is nearly always discussed in hushed whispers, so your child probably knows already that AIDS is something terrible, and may be scared. He wants both truth and reassurance. Children may also be confused about the difference and relationship between HIV and AIDS, which are frequently confused by adults as well.

GUIDELINES FOR YOUR ANSWERS

- Try not to be homophobic. Don't blame AIDS on gays or bisexual people, or let your child believe that only gay men get AIDS. Most newly reported HIV-positive cases are from heterosexual contacts, though most HIV-positive people in the US, Europe, and Australia are homosexual men. In Africa and Asia, AIDS is mainly a heterosexual problem.
- You will have to explain the difference between being HIV-positive and having full-blown AIDS, and know something about how the virus behaves, how it can be treated, and how it causes death. This background information will help, and it is much better for you to do a little homework to become better informed.
- Although HIV is a virus, it is not contagious like the common cold or flu. It's much harder to catch HIV – only a "pathological" dose, found in semen, blood, and possibly vaginal fluid, will infect a person.
- Emphasize the need for safe sex – wearing a condom for sex, unless you are in a monogamous relationship. Explain that a woman has the right to insist that a man wears a condom or not to have sex at all.

- Explain that AIDS is an extremely serious condition, but make it clear that there is no need to avoid contact with people who are HIV-positive or who have AIDS.

WHAT ELSE TO KNOW

- AIDS stands for Acquired Immune Deficiency Syndrome; HIV stands for Human Immunodeficiency Virus. Once a person has sufficient virus in the body, antibodies are produced and these can be picked up on testing – the test is "positive" for antibodies, and the person is said to be "HIV-positive."
- Most researchers believe that infection with HIV leads to the eventual breakdown of the body's immune system, leading to AIDS. This means the body is unable to defend itself against infections, leading eventually to death. There presently is no reliable cure for AIDS.

People can contract HIV from sexual intercourse with infected partners.

Other things you may be asked

- *Can you get AIDS from kissing?*
- *Can you get AIDS from shaking hands?*
- *Can you tell when someone's got AIDS?*
- *Can you get AIDS from going to the bathroom?*

See also *What is sex? p. 18* ● *What does it mean if you're "gay?" p. 36* ● *What happens when you die? p. 40*

Children under six are unlikely to ask this question because they probably won't come across AIDS at this age. If the subject does arise say, "AIDS is a serious illness that makes people sick for a long time. It can even kill people. You won't die of it – you won't even get it."

AIDS is a very serious disease. It's caused by a virus called HIV, which stands for Human Immunodeficiency Virus. After someone catches the virus, the person can have a blood test done which comes up "positive" – so the person is called "HIV-positive." The virus is mostly in people's blood, or their sperm if they're men, so it is difficult to catch it – mostly people only catch it now if sperm with the virus in it got into their bodies, if they're drug addicts sharing needles, or if they had a bad blood transfusion. But in most countries you can't get it from blood transfusions anymore because all blood is tested to make sure it's safe. Anyone could catch HIV, but most people don't because they are very careful. Very few children get AIDS; it sometimes happens if a woman was HIV-positive while a baby was growing in her tummy. Not many children die of AIDS. When people get the virus, at first they haven't got full-blown AIDS, but so far nearly every grown-up who's HIV-positive has eventually gotten AIDS, even though it takes as long as ten years. But while someone is just HIV-positive he may not be ill much at all, and can live normally.

HIV can only infect you from blood or semen. You can't get infected with HIV from going to the toilet, or swimming, or shaking hands, or from kissing or drinking from the same cup, so you can kiss and hug people with HIV or AIDS. In fact people with AIDS especially need hugs and love and kindness, because they will die as a result of having the virus. HIV damages the body's immune system – the way it fights diseases. If the immune system doesn't work, the body gives in to any germs that come along. AIDS is really the name for the whole list of symptoms and diseases a person with HIV is vulnerable to. HIV is normally passed on during sex because there are more viruses in semen than anything else. Men can pass it on to women or other men. Lesbians who have never had sex with a man don't usually get AIDS. But HIV also gets passed between drug users who share needles to inject themselves. When people have sex, men should always wear a condom, which prevents the virus being passed to the other person in semen. This is part of "safer sex," which means having sex in a way that stops HIV and other infections from being passed on.

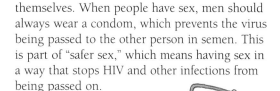

INDEX

Acknowledgments

Dorling Kindersley would like to thank:

Annette O'Sullivan for design assistance; Sarah Ashun for assisting the photographer; Wendy Holmes for makeup; Daisy Hayden for research; Elaine Harries for editorial assistance; Hilary Bird for the index

and the following children for modeling:

Ellie Blancke (2), Chrystell Brett (7), Stephanie Brett (4), Cassie Clarke (10), Daniel Clarke (7),William Duffus (8), Holly Durkin (5), Lauren Fernandez (4), Emily Gorton (6), Kashi Gorton (9), Shanti Gorton (4), Ethne Grey-Still (4) Thomas Greene (7), Thomas Holme (3), Megan Lacock (3), Claire Leonard (9), Lydia Leonard (9), Megan Leonard (6), Mitchell Leonard (3), Daniel Lord (4), Maija Marsh (7), Hayley Miles (2), Farid Mohamed (4), George Shellabear (4), Miriam Shellabear (2), Rebecca Shilling (10), Matthew Smith (10), Amy Walton (5), Calam West (9), Kera West (7).